WRITING:

The Powerful Healer

A collection of inspiring works about the amazing benefits of healing through words and the impact it has on the mind, body, and soul.

Copyright © 2015 by Christie Lyons & Jessie Welsh

All rights reserved. This book or any portion thereof may not be reproduced or used in any manner whatsoever without the express written permission of the publisher except for the use of brief quotations in a book review.

Printed in Australia

First Printing, 2015

ISBN 978-0-9925202-5-0

White Light Publishing House
25 Gretel Grove
Melton, VIC, Australia 3337

www.whitelightpublishingau.com

ABOUT WHITE LIGHT PUBLISHING HOUSE

White Light Publishing House aspires to share inspiration, guidance and love with the world, and to heal the mind, body and soul with words.

<u>www.whitelightpublishingau.com</u>

White Light Publishing House was established in 2014 by sisters, Christie and Jessie, who also co-run Soul Sistas Healing & Guidance. They have already have several books published including their own children's books as well as the inspirational works of other writers.

ACKNOWLEDGEMENTS

We would like to say a very heartfelt thank you to all of the amazing souls who have contributed to this book. We hope to be able to publish many more compilations like this one in the future; doing our part to raise awareness of mental health and sharing with the world just how helpful it is to express oneself creatively during this journey we call life.

A special thank you goes out to Karen McDermott, who not only provided us with a wonderful submission for this book, but inspired the both of us to write about our very own life journeys and publishing our stories in her books, 'Journey to Inner Light', and 'Living a Positive Life'. Karen also gave us the courage to move forward in creating our very own publishing company.

We are both extremely grateful to have been given this opportunity in life and to have found ourselves in a place where we are able to help others. We will continue to do so with the utmost passion. ♥

"To write is to bleed words onto the page – to be entirely vulnerable – the surest way to criticism and the clearest path to metamorphic transformation."

THIS BOOK IS DEDICATED TO OUR HUSBANDS, WHO HAVE BOTH HAD THEIR FAIR SHARE OF HARDSHIPS, TRAUMA AND CHALLENGES IN THEIR LIVES, AND HAVE HAD THE COURAGE TO WORK THROUGH THEM. ♥

"People who engage in expressive writing report feeling happier and less negative than before writing. Similarly, reports of depressive symptoms, rumination, and general anxiety tend to drop in the weeks and months after writing about emotional upheavals."

From "Writing to Heal" by James W Pennebaker

CONTENTS

PAGE

INTRODUCTION	15
ABOUT THERAPEUTIC WRITING	19
WORK IN PROGRESS – AMANDA SCHUBERT	23
POETRY BY RANDALL FOSS	27
WRITING POSSIBLY SAVED MY LIFE – TAMIKA DAWSON	43
BACK TO ME – CHRISTIE LYONS	49
WRITE TO BE FREE – LOUISE GINGLO	59
ALEX – LANI SHARP	83
HEALING THE WRITE WAY - KAREN MCDERMOTT	95
POETRY & MORE – ELLA KATE REEVES	115
WRITE IT OUT…IT REALLY WORKS! – JESSIE WELSH	145
RIGHT TO HEAL – SHAUNA NORMAN	151
ARTICLES	171
USEFUL RESOURCES AND LINKS	223

"Write hard and clear about what hurts."

Ernest Hemingway

WRITING:

The Powerful Healer

A collection of inspiring works about the amazing benefits of healing through words and the impact it has on the mind, body, and soul.

"Writing is a form of therapy; sometimes I wonder how all those who do not write, compose, or paint can manage to escape the madness, melancholia, the panic and fear which is inherent in a human situation."

Graham Greene

INTRODUCTION

Both Christie and Jessie have personally experienced the benefits of healing through writing and know exactly how therapeutic and empowering it is to be able to express themselves on paper in order to begin the healing process.

With the assistance of their dear friend Karen McDermott, they were both lucky enough to be able to write their own personal stories and have them published in compilations published by Serenity Press and both Christie and Jess are very grateful to Karen for encouraging them to share their journeys publicly.

After having their own stories published, and with the encouragement of Karen, Christie and Jessie went on to establish their very own publishing company, as they both very soon realised that they had many more stories to tell, as well as an abundance of ideas for children's books. One thing that stood out to both of them was that they would like to be able to extend upon their work through Soul Sistas Healing, and give others the opportunity to share their stories and talents, and have their own work published.

Among many other things that Christie and Jessie have in common, they have both experienced what it is like to have several people very close to them in their lives suffer from a mental illness; as well as Christie having suffered from depression and anxiety herself. For this reason, they are both advocates for the brilliant work that Beyond Blue carry out, and wish to be able to help those who suffer from this silent illness in any way they can.

After finding how therapeutic it was for both of them to write about their life journey thus far, they decided to develop this book. Christie and Jessie accepted submissions from everyday people about how writing has helped them in their lives, and even encouraged people to practice it for themselves for the very first time, to be able to experience therapeutic writing firsthand, which you will see reflected in some of the stories that have been included in this book.

The aim of publishing this compilation of stories is to help people become aware of the wonderful benefits of healing through writing and just how very powerful it can be. ♥

ABOUT THERAPEUTIC WRITING

Firstly, let us explore what we mean when we talk about 'writing'. Writing encompasses many things, and is not simply limited to writing a story, but can cover several different forms of using words, such as:

- Poetry
- Song/lyrics
- Journaling
- Blogging
- Writing articles
- Letter writing

It is very important to note that each person will have their own unique way of expressing themselves, and it all depends upon what feels right for the individual. Of course, some people prefer other creative outlets such as dance, playing music, or artwork (but we'll save that for another book!)

It doesn't matter which form of expression you choose; each one has wonderful healing benefits, and it's not so much about what is being written, but how it affects you; both while you're writing, and afterwards. You should choose how you wish to express yourself based on what feels more comfortable for you. It may even be a mixture of different formats.

A vital aspect of using writing as a therapeutic tool is to be as honest as you can with yourself, and just allow the words to flow. It doesn't matter if you have spelling or grammatical errors, or whether it makes sense to anyone else. What matters is that YOU have been able to let the words out. Along with releasing those words (whether you realise it initially or not), you will have also freed any thoughts and emotions that are attached to those words.

You may feel anger, frustration, grief, or even physically ill while going through this process, but know that these feelings are ones that will shed along with your words. These words and emotions that you've been holding onto and causing you so much pain can very quickly shift from being attached to you and your mental state, to words that can help another, just by expressing them through writing.

So, what are you waiting for? Start your writing journey now and you'll see the benefits for yourself!

"Tell your story: Yes, tell your story. Show your example. Tell everyone it's possible, and others shall feel the courage to climb their own mountains."

Paul Coelho

WORK IN PROGRESS

By Amanda Schubert

The first time I realised the power of writing was when I was eight years old, and I had just finished reading 'Black Beauty' by Anna Sewell for the first time. I was too young then to understand exactly what had happened, but I knew that reading that book had changed me. There were many concepts I couldn't grasp in that initial read, but the empathy I'd felt for Beauty was real. The emotions that Anna's words had brought out in me were real. The magic was real.

Over the years, 'Black Beauty' has always had a special place in my heart. It will forever be the book that woke me up to the power of writing; the power to reach into another person's heart and touch their lives deeply, without ever meeting them. I knew that I wanted to be a writer; that I wanted to open people's minds and hearts with my words. What I hadn't expected was the way this power would affect my own life.

As a student, I was always terrible at public speaking; I would mutter and mumble, too shy to speak up and articulate my words. My teachers would constantly pull me up for racing when reading aloud, as I tried to spit the words out at the same speed that my mind read them (I have always had a mind that races faster than my mouth ever could!). No, verbal communication was never my strong point…and still isn't! As I grew older, a lot more of my school assignments revolved around writing stories or essays then reading them aloud to the class. The writing part for me was easy – words flow through my fingers much better than they flow from my mouth! I used to get very good scores for my written essays. However, when it came time to read them aloud to the class, I used to feel ill; all of my work felt like a part of me, my thoughts, my opinions, and now

I needed to share that with my peers, many who would just ignore it or, worse, laugh? No thank you! At the time, I never realised why sharing my written work bothered me so much. Now, as a young adult, I understand; it came from the heart, and I wasn't ready to share my heart with just anybody!

Whenever I was confronted with feelings I couldn't express verbally, I would always put it in writing. The times I asked boys on dates, they received letters. Letters to resolve arguments, letters to explain my point of view to someone, letters to show my appreciation. It was as if my hands could express my feelings better than my mouth ever could; I was always the most genuine and honest when I was writing. This used to annoy some people, who would ask why I couldn't just talk to them, why I had to say everything in writing. I couldn't explain to them what it was; I just preferred to write it all down.

Looking back on those childhood and teenage years, I now see why it was so hard for me to express myself through the spoken word. I am an introvert, and an Empath. I see and feel so much, and so deeply, that the emotions often feel too strong for words. Speaking is not something that I find easy to do, and I still struggle to this day. I speak too quickly, I jumble my words, and I am always afraid of saying something 'the wrong way'. But writing…oh, writing is my escape, my release! Where my mouth fails to keep up with my mind, my hands and my fingers somehow manage to get the words out as I think them. If I do stumble or make a mistake, a simple line or hit of the delete button and it all makes sense again; no stuttering my words and confusing and embarrassing myself!

I didn't have a bad childhood, or a terribly traumatic one, but one thing that affected me very deeply and has left a huge emotional scar, was being bullied throughout my school years. I was a very shy and sensitive child (being the introvert that I am!) and there were others who used to take advantage of this and tease me, calling me names and laughing at me. Naturally, this served to make me even more quiet and shy, and so the cycle continued. Even now, as an adult, I still worry endlessly about the opinions of others, and whether they will laugh at me or call me names. It gave me terrible social anxiety; if my family went to get take-away, or to the local football games, I would have to stay in the car, I would refuse to get out in case someone saw me and made fun of me. I distinctly remember an incident where my mother, one of my two younger sisters, and I went to watch my youngest sister perform in a concert at the local theatre. My mother, who is a wonderful, outgoing, and vibrant woman, was dancing along to the music and cheering loudly for my little sister. I was so worried that someone would look at us and laugh at us, that I told her to stop embarrassing me…but secretly, I wanted to dance with her. I really hurt my mother's feelings that day. Suddenly, this wasn't just my problem anymore; my anxiety was hurting people I loved.

During the years between leaving school and the present, it got a little easier; I had some wonderful friends who were always there to lift me out of the gloom of depression when I sank too low, and who offered me love and support without judgement. I also had the love and support of my family, which has never wavered. I was beginning to heal; I began to feel a sense of worth again. I was more than I had been made to believe by those bullies in school, and I had something special to offer the world. But that black cloud of anxiety, that depression, was always there in the background, just waiting for the slightest chink to appear in the armour my friends and family provided. All it would take was a small argument with a friend, and it would be back – that despair, those feelings of worthlessness and insecurity.

For all the external love I had, I still hadn't mended the broken pieces inside.

In 2009, I married my first boyfriend, my love, and my life-partner. I had never known what it felt like to be wanted by someone, to be loved by someone the way Daniel loved me, and it went a long way to healing my old scars. Our daughter was born in 2010, and our son soon followed in 2012. Both were born via Caesarean after complications, and while I believed I had convinced myself that it didn't matter how they were delivered as long as we were all healthy, I couldn't help but feel like I had 'failed' somehow. I actively avoided parenting forums, and discussions about vaginal births vs Caesar's. I could feel the cracks opening again; those old feelings of self-loathing and not being 'good enough'.

I knew I needed to do something about the anxiety and depression. It was affecting my life more and more each day. Having children is, without a doubt, the greatest thing I have ever done in my life, but it also brought out many insecurities. There are so many ideas and beliefs about what being a 'good parent' is, that I began to worry constantly that I was doing it wrong; I was bombarded daily with thoughts like, "What if someone sees me feeding my baby girl formula? They'll think I'm a terrible mother! Don't they understand that my milk dried up at three months and I can't breastfeed?" "My son can't walk yet, but he's two years old…I'd better not take him to the playground in case someone is mean to us. How can I explain that he has a chromosomal duplication that means he's delayed in speech and walking, but he's still a bright and fun-loving child? No one will take the time to understand – they will all just laugh at us and think I'm an awful mother!" My whole family was suffering because of my issues. It had to stop.

I tried counselling, but that was a huge failure. Not because of my therapist, he was wonderful. The problem was, just as I had been in school, I was terrible at expressing my thoughts and feelings verbally. I would try to explain the issues I was having, but would end up jumbling my words, stuttering, and then feeling too embarrassed to continue talking. No, counselling was not the right therapy for me. I needed a different way to release the emotions, to express my anxiety and fear in order to let it go and move on. It was around this time I decided to explore my spiritual side a little more in-depth. During my studies into alternative and spiritual therapies, I came across information about release ceremonies. This immediately resonated with me, and I decided to try it for myself.

Release ceremonies involve writing down anything and everything you wish to let go of, then either tearing it up, burying it or burning it, to send the negative energy away. So, one full moon, I conducted my first release ceremony. From the moment my pen touched the paper, I knew that this was the key to undoing the knots that had built up in my soul. I could not write fast enough. In the end, my words were completely illegible, but it didn't matter. As I wrote, I felt each and every emotion surface from within my subconscious and flow out through my hand onto the paper. I wrote about being bullied, I wrote about my parents' divorce, I wrote about my feelings of failure at not having natural births, I wrote out every dark and terrible thing that had ever happened to me. I lost track of time completely; it was as if I had turned on a tap that had been long rusted and there was no stopping the flow until it was all gone. By the time I finished purging all the built-up emotions, my fingers were numb and my hand was cramped. The pages in my notebook were full of scribbles and tearstains. I was completely drained.

And it felt wonderful.

There, on the pages, was my anxiety and depression in writing. Everything that I had kept built up inside, that I had never been able to express through spoken words, was on those pages. Writing had opened up the doors and let it all out. It was with a huge sigh of relief that I set fire to those pages that night. I knew I wasn't completely healed, that some scars went deeper still, but I had finally found a way to express it all, to sort through the jumble and unravel the knots. It was the beginning of a long road to healing.

These days, I use writing as a daily therapy. When things feel overwhelming, I sit down and write. Sometimes I write down my feelings just to get them out of me. Other times, I write something completely unrelated as a distraction when I am feeling anxious or nervous. I write lists, I write poems, I write letters or stories…I just write. The person I am now is barely recognisable as the quiet, timid child I was. Sure, I still worry about what others think of me, and I still have fears about not being 'good enough', but they are manageable. When it gets too much, I simply write down a list of all the things I am grateful for, or the things I like about myself, and that gives me a bit of a boost! Writing has released the person I had buried beneath the dark cloud of anxiety, depression, and unworthiness. It is still my aim to one day write my own novel, and let my words flow from my heart into the hearts of others, just as Anna Sewell did for me with 'Black Beauty' all those years ago. I'd just about given up on that idea, convincing myself that nobody would care about what I had to say. But now, well…I'll let writing do the speaking for me.

POETRY

By Randall Foss

My name is Randall Foss. I'm 30 years old and I live in Massachusetts. I've always been drawn to the mystical power of words, especially when they are arranged with artistic design. I personally believe in the healing capabilities of composing and enjoying written works and I hope to make a positive impact on people's lives with my creations.

Puzzles

I yearn to express these thoughts that I think

They're driving me wild

They spill like my ink

My ink through the pen like blood through my veins

The magic of process

To tell what became

Became of my visions so patiently placed

On paper or screen

To set up the place

The place where I'll take you to lose your own mind

Develop a picture

No concept of time

There's no expedition that makes me feel free

--

Like dragging the pencil

Or striking the keys

The puzzles of language have brought me such peace

A bright satisfaction

A love spell unleashed

A rhythmic relation where heart meets the soul

Compelling their voices

Adventures untold

This beautiful bondage to portraits unseen

A cradle of comfort

A kiss to my dreams

Just a Pen

It's not just a pen
It's a wand I propel
To cast out the voices
With stories to tell

It's not just a surface
With scratches and scrapes
It's powerful monuments
Chiseled in faith

It's not just some words
Of letters arranged
They're framework to images
Softly explained

It's not just a line
To ponder again
It's here to remind you
It's not just a pen

WRITING POSSIBLY SAVED MY LIFE

By Tamika Dawson

I first started writing this piece with a specific time of my life in mind, where I used writing as a way to cope, to understand, and to heal. However, I then thought about other periods of my life, and realised I had used writing in the same way then as well; just in different modes. As a child and early teenager, I used to write fiction. I would make up stories; some short, some long. Some of them I made into short series. Today I look back and ask myself if there was a reason as to why I turned to writing at that time, and whilst I did not realise it until now, there was.

I don't really remember much of my childhood in terms of events that happened, but I remember feeling sad and not fitting in with family and friends. I realised today that I turned to writing at that time of my life to perhaps create something exciting to the characters that wasn't happening in my own life at the time. It didn't matter that I didn't have friends, because I could come home from school and write my own stories where the characters *did* have friends, and were happy. I think I created the lives of the characters as how I wished my life was at the time.

I remember writing in a journal, and then typing journal entries on my laptop, when I was a teenager. Looking back this was a period right before I fell into deep depression and had the early signs of a quickly escalating, life-threatening eating disorder. I no longer have those entries, as one night, in the middle of the night, when I wasn't sure if I was going to wake up the next morning, I ripped up and threw away the written entries and deleted the typed ones from my computer, because I didn't want to die and have my parents read through them afterwards. This tells me there would have been something in those entries that I obviously didn't want them to know, but something I obviously felt the need to write about anyway.

I did wake up that next morning, but not long afterwards, I spent my first ever hospital admission in the Children's Ward of the hospital for treatment of anorexia. This first admission was for four weeks and I was fed by a tube to help me put on weight. It was during this admission that I started to write poetry. Sometimes I wrote more than one a day. The words in the poems told my story of how I was feeling at the time; how much I hated myself; how no one understood me or what I was going through; how "I didn't want to be here anymore". I didn't relay any of this to my family, friends, nurses, or psychologist and dietician who were seeing me at the time, but I wrote it all down. The poems themselves were obviously quite depressing, though it helped me to get out what I was feeling at the time; what I couldn't speak in words to anyone around me.

I had a few short hospital admissions after that, and then another lengthy admission, of twelve weeks, in a child and adolescent psychiatric unit after my first suicide attempt, where I was mainly treated for my anorexia, and was only 24-48 hours away from a few vital organs failing. I continued to write poetry during this period too.

After this I completed High School and went onto University. I don't think I wrote much then, except for assignments, but I put my whole soul into my studies, and achieved very good grades, but I wonder now if this was also a coping mechanism I used via writing, as life wasn't great at that time either.

I ended up getting married, and had my husband leave me for my best friend nearly eight months ago. I also lost my job a few short weeks later. Suddenly I found myself lost again. I didn't turn to writing in the traditional sense at this time, though I read many inspirational quotes, and made some of my own, and am in the middle of putting these together and making a book of quotes for me to read, if I ever get really down and need to be uplifted again. I have also kept in touch with friends, mostly via e-mail or private messages, during this time as well. I get to hear about their lives, and they mine, and this makes me feel less alone in this world, and to gain courage and inspiration to keep moving forward.

Looking back over my past, and the different times in my life, where I have used writing in different modes, makes me wonder how my future with writing will pan out. I really believe writing has helped me through some very dark patches in my life, and possibly even saved my life a few times. I hope to use writing in my future, during happy times as well!

BACK TO ME

By Christie Lyons

I have always enjoyed writing; even from a very early age. My beloved grandfather would spend countless hours with me – helping and encouraging my love of words. It was no surprise then, that once I began primary school and was given the opportunity to start expressing myself through writing that I thrived. I was lucky enough to have a very inspirational and loving Grade One teacher, whom I still keep in contact with to this day. It was during my year with Mrs Carnell in particular where I started bringing home pieces of work – mostly poetry, but some short stories as well – some of which have been kept by my mother and grandmother for me to look back at now.

I maintained my interest in writing right up until the end of primary school, and even had a couple of my teachers tell me that they would be keeping their eye out in the future for my name printed on the front of books. For a long time as a child, when someone asked me what I wanted to be when I grew up, I would tell them I wanted to be an author – that was after I had it explained to me that being a 'book maker' wasn't in fact what I thought it was!

Somewhere along the line, between high school and my twenties, my dream of writing as a profession got pushed to the side, but I did start writing in a journal. Journaling was, and still is, something that has gotten me through some very challenging times; including heartbreak, trauma, relationships troubles, and most of all, helped me to work through and make sense of my anxiety and depression.

When I read back now over some of my journal entries, it amazes me to see how different I was back then, but also how far I've come. It's almost like I was a completely different person, and in some ways I was. When I flick from one year to another, there's evidence there of my progression through dealing with each challenge, and it makes me feel very proud of myself. Mind you, if someone else were ever to read them, they would likely think I was crazy!

That's the beauty of journaling however; it doesn't need to be for anyone else but me. I can rant, rave, express my deepest emotions, and be painfully honest, and I know that it's a safe place for me to do so, without anyone's judgement but my own. Everything just makes so much more sense once I've written it down, and this was particularly true in regards to when I was going through the toughest period of my anxiety. I would find myself writing down my thoughts and feelings when I was feeling very anxious, and once I had transferred them from my mind and onto the page, it helped me realise that my thoughts were just that: thoughts, and that in reality, everything was okay.

Another common occurrence for me is to write letters when I feel that I can't talk about an issue verbally. Often I do find it less confronting and much easier to express myself truthfully, when I can write it down and get my message across through a letter. I still use this technique at times with my husband, and it works well, because it means that he can read my letter in his own time, with no interruptions and respond when he is ready to. It is helpful because it allows us both to speak honestly, and resolve our problems relatively peacefully. Letter writing is not only a wonderful way to stay connected with loved ones (even though not many people do it anymore), but a great way to have that conversation with someone when you feel too uncomfortable or anxious about speaking to them in person. Another thing I sometimes do is write someone a letter to let my feelings out, but then burn or tear up the letter. The main purpose of me writing the letter is often for my own benefit, and not necessarily because I want the person to read it. It's a wonderful release.

Needless to say, after all those years of writing letters and journaling, I do have quite the collection. I can tell which years of my life were the most challenging just by looking at how many journals I had for that year. There are several years where I hadn't even kept one, and in fact, I haven't felt the need to write in a journal for the last few years, and I believe that is because I've found other ways to express myself through my writing; ways that are not so private, but still allow me to be open and honest, and at the same time, hopefully help someone else in the process.

Late 2012 was when my love for writing really made its way back into my life, and sadly, it took something tragic to occur for this to happen. Not long before Christmas, I found out the heartbreaking news that the baby I was carrying had died. It felt like my heart had been torn into a million pieces and I spent a long time afterwards, trying to make sense of it all. It was when I came across Karen McDermott's book, The Visitor, that things finally started to make sense to me, and every word in that book helped me to see my loss from a very different perspective. Shortly afterward, I decided to send a thank you message to the author of this beautiful book, and we got chatting about how our lives were similar in many ways. I told her of some of my experiences in life so far, and she suggested that I write about them. Karen was in the process of putting together a collection of inspirational stories, and encouraged me to contribute.

Well, I don't think I've ever gotten to work so quickly on something in my entire life! I had never considered doing anything like this before, even though I had told several people in the past that I could 'write a book' about my life, but it was always in a joking manner. I immediately felt a sense of purpose, and knew that the sooner I got to work on my story, that the healing process would begin for me. Little did I know however, just how much healing there was to be experienced; there were things I had experienced from many years ago that had remained buried for some time and it wasn't until I started writing about them that the feelings resurfaced and I realised just how very much I needed this. In particular there was a part of my life that I had written about which made me feel physically ill as I was writing the words, but I knew that this was my way of letting go of all the pain and heartache that I had unknowingly buried deep for many years.

My story was published in a book called 'Journey to Inner Light' and it was honest, raw, and the whole process changed my life. I finally felt free from all that I had held onto for so long. Not only did writing about my life's journey help me to heal, but it also reminded me how much I loved to write. After going through that process, my passion for expressing myself with words returned, and there was no stopping me! I began to have articles published on www.buildingbeautifulbonds.com and very soon afterwards, started up a publishing company with my sister in law Jess. After only a year, we already have some children's books of our own published and are helping others to get their work out there as well.

I have long believed that everything happens for a reason, and no matter what happens in life, you are always drawn back to your purpose and passions in life, even if it takes a while to get there.

WRITE TO BE FREE

By Louise Ginglo

I love writing. Words are powerful. They are emotions and thoughts scrawled onto paper in moments of anxiety, times of sadness, as an expulsion of anger, to organise confusion about a situation and to note all the beauty, magic and miracles this entire universe is responsible for.

Even though I am good at talking and I love a great conversation, I find that when I need to express myself, it flows better when I write. For example, when I am sad, I am able to go deeper into my feelings and let the words communicate exactly what it is that is upsetting me. When I am angry, I can clearly convey my frustration about a situation without my voice trembling and my eyes welling up with tears. When I want to get a point across or feel as though I have been treated unfairly in a situation, I feel completely comfortable writing a letter or an email with clear and concise content to the person or company in question and I can state what I feel in a direct, calm and polite manner.

Writing soothes me; I am able to get all the words and conversation that is creating noise in my mind onto paper and out of my body. My stress levels drop as I tell my story and I feel as though I have been heard, even if no one gets to read what I have written. I like to believe that my guardian angels, the universe or God, have listened to every single letter, every prayer, the poems, the pleas – everything! Once all of my feelings, my fears, any hurt and pain or sadness I feel, as well as my dreams, hopes and desires have been released, they are received by the big driving force that is beyond anything we can see. Everything is moving in the right direction for me to be led to exactly where I am meant to be.

When I was a teenager, I began singing lessons. I was passionate about singing, I was certain using my voice, and performing the songs I loved was going to be my way of expressing myself and finding the true me. I loved reading and interpreting the lyrics of songs – poems sung to music and open to interpretation. The more I could relate to the lyrics the more I loved the song and yearned to perform it.

By the end of high school and close to the age of eighteen, I started dating someone; this became my first long-term serious relationship. It did not take long for me to be absolutely smitten with this guy. I loved him and believed he was The One…I was wrong. Not long into our relationship, he broke up with me and I was devastated; I cried for days. I needed a way to express myself, so I started a journal. I poured all of my emotions onto the pages with real tears included, still staining the pages to this very day.

We got back together many times and we broke up many times. Everything about him and our relationship was unpredictable. There were the times when it was all going smoothly, "I love you" was being said; I was happy, I believed he was happy and then without warning he would stop talking to me. It went something like this; Sunday morning we would go for a romantic walk on the beach, by Sunday night he wouldn't be talking to me. All affection would be shut off and there was a distinct wall between us – no touching, no hugging, no kissing – nothing. He would then leave and go home. I would be left standing there wondering what on earth it was I had done to deserve this form of punishment. What did I do, that was so bad that he felt compelled to ignore me, and feel the intense need to get away from me? Every time he did this to me, I would spend days writing in my journal, it was the only way for me to have a voice. I would question why he did this to me but of course, my letters didn't provide me with an answer - I did it because writing it all down and getting it out of my bewildered mind, helped me to feel better. My words were my friend and they were healing me when I was so lost and mystified by my boyfriends' actions.

Whenever he did this to me, I wouldn't hear from him for weeks. When he finally did contact me, it was to tell me he wanted to break up, yet again. This led to more journaling. I was frustrated and angry as to why he couldn't have spared me all the extra pain and been honest in the first place, rather than have me in limbo for days, or weeks.

My journaling then turned to poetry and lyric writing. Singing had always been my passion, and yet when I was in this frame of mind, I couldn't sing…so I thought writing lyrics for songs would be my next avenue. While my heart bled, my creative mind combined the words together to reveal my hurt, my frustration and my pain; and in doing this, my soul was being healed.

Here is one of the poems I wrote around the time of 1996 when I was 23. It won't win any prizes for being a great poem, but I was writing from the heart and it is evident I was beginning to come to terms with the fact that my on and off relationship had put me through years of anguish and it was finally coming to an end.

She stands at the water, the waves coming in at her feet,

Watching the sun rise and wondering where the hell she has been.

He told her of this plans, of how they should go away together.

It will be so much fun, let's go today!

And she wonders where the hell they've been.

And do you love me? Like you tell me you do.

Do you love me? Let's make it work this time.

Can you love me, the way you used to?

And as she stands at the water, with the soft sand between her toes,

Looking out to her future, where to now? I don't know?

Do you love me? You said you still do.

Do you love me? It'll be better this time round.

Yeah you love me, just not the way you used to.

And so he tells her once again, that the time is still not right.

And her heart is broken again, she won't sleep tonight.

The turmoil I went through from this relationship was a lifetime ago. I am grateful I was able to write about it at the time and I believe it helped me get through everything I was experiencing. I was able to re-read what I had written and see it from a new perspective, assess myself and discover what it was I expected not only from someone else in a relationship but also from myself. In doing this I believe I was able to heal quicker than I would have had I let everything boil up inside of me but never quite let it come up to the surface and spill out. The good thing about keeping it all as a journal was that I never needed to worry about whether I was a good writer or not – it didn't matter because the only one reading my words, was me. I could get as angry as I wanted, use as many swear words I wanted, describe my boyfriend (or ex, depending on the time it was written) using judgmental words, because it was personal and it was for my eyes only. I am now blessed and grateful to have a husband who treats me with respect and has never once chosen to ignore me for weeks on end and then break up with me.

My writing has evolved in many ways over the past twenty-something years or so, reaching new levels to help me through other areas of my life. About ten years ago when I desperately wanted to lose weight, I used a journal to write about the challenges I faced with weight loss, as well as my issues with my body. In doing this, I was able to recognize when I was prone to emotional eating and why I felt the need to indulge in junk food. The journal also helped me to assess where I needed to improve with my diet and lifestyle.

Using a journal for weight loss gave me the ultimate opportunity to be as upfront with myself as possible about my body image. Seeing the negative words I used to describe myself in my journal, shocked me. I could clearly see just how unkind I was about my own body. I would never describe a friend as ugly, fat or hideous, and yet here I was using these very words to describe myself.

I made a promise to myself to focus on my beauty – even if I could only find one thing at a time. For example, 'I love my thin hands', 'I love the colour of my eyes' or 'I have a radiant smile.' Writing it down, made it feel real. It wasn't just a fleeting thought, it was there on paper for me to acknowledge and accept.

Writing while on my weight loss journey truly did bring about my success. I was able to slow down and focus on the core meaning of what losing weight was all about for me. I became aware that losing weight was important for my health - in body, mind and spirit. Losing weight was no longer about being thin, or fitting into skinny jeans, or lusting after that little black dress. It was about stripping away all the unhealthy baggage I carried around and discovering the healthier me – the whole healthy package.

My next goal was to write a book. Writing the book was healing for me. I was able to release a lot of the pain and frustration I felt from years of feeling unworthy because I was overweight, as well as the disappointment I had in myself for not being able to follow diets and experience weight loss success. It was important for me to write a story that was mine, but it was also a story that is familiar to so many others; which is why I wrote the book in story form with a character, rather than making it into a memoir. It is a story so many people can relate to.

The book is about a woman who has struggled with her weight for many years and has been on diet after diet. With many weight loss failures up her sleeve, she decides to give up dieting and focus on her health. With the assistance of a Healthy Lifestyle Coach, she goes on a journey to discovering herself. She uncovers her beauty and her belief in herself, resulting in her unleashing a healthier version of who she is. Not only did I find therapy in writing my book, but also my aim was to also help others change their perspective about dieting, so they can go on their own journey to leading a fulfilling healthy lifestyle.

I am passionate about helping people find an abundance of love for their own self. We are so hard on ourselves and who we are. We become lost in a world of competing and comparing. We put all of our love into others and we so easily forget about the most important person in the world - The Self.

When I write, at first, it truly is for me. I write about past experiences - with my emotions and feelings attached. I write about challenges I currently face to get it out of my system and see me through – but I also write about things that other people have opened up to me about. When people talk to me, I find myself in their shoes for that period of time and I am then able to later translate it into a story…I bring back their emotions and I put it all on paper. I believe that in doing this I can help many people. Too often, we feel completely alone with our feelings, our heartache and our drama. It is a relief to read a story that sounds like our own, but it has come from someone else, and you become aware, that you are not alone with your own story; others are treading a similar path.

Here is just one of the short stories I have posted on my Facebook page about True Love:

Her True Love

I step into the room and intuitively I can feel their energy. All of them are here waiting for their loved one to walk through the door so they can deliver their messages and assure them that they are okay and at peace now.

I sit down across from the woman who is a channel for these souls – they know of her gift and swarm to her with excitement and anticipation about communicating with the physical world again.

I can sense the softness in her core, but she wears a hard shell – she has to be like this – it is the only way for her to convey what she hears – and always with honesty.

"What is it you want to know?" She asks me. There is one question I have; I will be asking about the one thing I have been searching for, for so long. "When will I find my one and only true love?" I ask, with much urgency and neediness, because it is all I want out of my life.

"Your true love is already here." She says gently to me. "The love that this person has for you is eternal. It is so deep and so pure – all that is left now is for you to recognize this love, accept the love and embrace your love."

I listen with intent as she talks about this person who is going to love me so much. I am wondering who this person is, that is so close to me and yet I am unaware of how much they love me.

"Take a look into my crystal ball and there you will see the vision of your true love."

I do as she asks, but all I see is my reflection. There is no image of a tall, dark handsome prince coming to sweep me off my feet.

"SHE is your true love." She says to me, answering my query about the absence of another person.

"When your mind accepts the love of your soul, your heart will be captured forever. Once you have discovered this true love, and allow it to envelope your whole being, it will never leave you. This is the kind of love that opens your eyes to everything."

It never occurred to me that I was my true love. I was so wrapped up in finding someone else out there to love me and accept me for all that I am, that I neglected to acknowledge my own souls love. I thought that love was reserved for someone else.

"Take another look into my crystal ball." She says smiling at me.

I look into the divination tool that sits in front of me and this time, my reflection is glowing – I am more beautiful than ever. I see visions of me united with my true love – we have strength, courage, acceptance, respect, trust, and kindness. We get through the lessons in life together and have the power to quash bad energy and the capacity to inhale a mass of healthy energy.

I am confident I will never accept another being to just be in my life in order to fill a void – because with my true love, there are no holes that need to be filled - no emptiness, only fulfilment.

I am grateful for the message that was passed on to me from a loved one who is in spirit and I am blessed to have discovered my eternal true love.

When I post the short stories or quotes I have written, people send me a private message or comment about how they feel as though I have read their mind. They thank me for putting all of their thoughts and feelings into a new perspective and shining some light on an area of darkness. I have also encouraged others who I know are going through tough times to write in their own way about what is happening in their life. Those who have tried it, agree that it is a huge relief to get their story out of them – whether it's a journal, a blog or poetry.

The next short story is one I posted on my personal page. It was also published in an e-magazine after being well received on a Facebook community page aimed at wellness and healthy eating.

Her Reflection

"You are so fat. You're ugly too." She says, while standing in front of the mirror, staring at her reflection. "Look at this! Your stomach is flabby and big. Your thighs are chunky and your arms have big wings." Her eyes then settle on her face. "I wish I looked like the actress in that movie I watched last night. A natural beauty – hardly any make-up on her face and she was stunning. But you! You look white, pale and tired. Your eyes are uneven, and they aren't even a nice colour. You have thin lips a double chin and a pointy nose. No amount of make-up will hide these flaws. I hate looking at you."

She flops onto the bed, feeling helpless, knowing there is nothing she can do about her appearance. She will never look like that actress. She knew it was possible to change her body, if she was to get herself into action and actually follow that diet she keeps talking about and do some exercise. But her face, that can never change – it is what it is, and unfortunately it's not pretty.

"Okay, that's enough!" She heard a voice from somewhere in the room yelling at her. She jumps up in fright, wondering where on earth that voice just came from. "All you do is put me down and talk about how fat and ugly I am – and honestly, I am over it." She couldn't believe what her eyes were seeing; her reflection was still standing in the mirror and was talking to her.

"Do you know how much it hurts to hear you throw insults my way, every time you look at me? You stand there and spit out negative and mean words, one after the other and it makes me angry." She knew her reflection had a point. She didn't admire anything she saw in the mirror - everything to her was ugly and full of flaws. "But what do I do? Everything I am saying is true. Don't you agree?"

"If you choose to see only ugliness then I guess YOU believe that your words are true. But I don't see it like that at all. Look at our legs; you think they are chunky, but I see strength and mobility. You think our arms are unsightly because they have wings; I see hugs that are full of love and hands that wave when you meet loved ones or extend to a shake when meeting someone new." "You focus on our rolls of fat; but I see healthy curves. Take a good look at our smile..." Her reflection smiles at her – it is friendly and warm. "This is what people see when you greet them."

"You think your face is pale; I see a delicate porcelain complexion. You look tired because you are never excited to see me. You are unhappy with our dark and brooding eyes; I can go deeper, and I am touched by a beautiful soul. Our eyes are alluring. They are full of love, kindness and compassion toward others; but why not for you – me – us?"

Her reflection made her see things she had never seen before. Her reflection told her things she had never heard before. Her reflection will never be perfect but SHE found beauty, where she could only see ugliness.

She was starting to see what her image was reflecting back at her. Her eyes softened as she took in everything that stood in front of her in this crystal clear mirror. She knew it was time to look into her true self and focus on her beauty as a whole. She now smiles at her reflection with love and only speaks to her with words of kindness.

Writing is personal; it is an intimate conversation between you, the pen and paper or the keyboard and a file on your computer. When you choose to note down all of your thoughts it is therapeutic for your soul, soothing for your body as you release pent-up stress and emotions and calming as you turn down the volume on the noise in your mind and let it scream with drama and passion on paper.

I never thought of myself as a writer, and I certainly never thought I would go as far as writing a book and publishing it, or write short stories and allow other people to read them. Once I let go of my fears and doubts about myself as a writer, I opened myself up and wrote from my heart. The more I write, the more creative I become; the more creative I become, the more I heal myself in ways I never believed possible.

ALEX

By Lani Sharp

Gnome: *noun* - A legendary dwarfish creature, supposed to guard the Earth's treasures; diminutive spirits or small fey 'humanoids' in Renaissance magic and alchemy, first introduced by Paracelsus in the 16th century, known for their eccentric sense of humour, inquisitiveness, and engineering prowess; are typically said to be a small, humanoid creature that live underground.

I first met Alex when I was seven. He was to change the course of my creative life. Born with a fertile imagination, an insatiable curiosity and a natural affinity with Earth spirits and 'other worlds', both my parents encouraged the development of this by believing me when I told them I had a new friend, a gnome, Alex, who lived in the lush garden just beyond our front door.

I was also this tender age when I learned that my dad, a highly imaginative and right-brain-oriented person himself, was dying of a brain tumour and only had a limited time left with us. For as long as I could remember, he had been like my doorway to this other world, and losing him meant that this door might close forever. I was afraid, sad, alone, frightened, confused, all at the same time at this prospect of losing my doorway into that place where the grass was always greener, the inhabitants friendly and joy abounded. It was tough too, never knowing if this day or that hour or that afternoon, might be the last time I ever spent time with my treasured father. Every day I - we - lived on edge, with an ominous cloud of uncertainty hanging over us.

Then Alex entered my life. I received a beautiful shiny, soft-covered, thick book all about gnomes and I fell in love with these cheeky little creatures! I read the book day and night, revelling in its vivid pictures and detailed descriptions. The book informed me all about gnomes' habitats, where they could be 'found', their lifestyles, their clothes, what they ate, what type of pets they lived with, what they did for fun, how they worked, and much, much more. A new world had opened up to me! It was like it had been inside me all along, this little ideal fantasyland, and now I finally had the key that unlocked the door that led right into it! The book became my bible, my bedside companion, the king of my bookshelf, and I read it whenever I had a spare moment, absorbing all the text and pictures with gusto.

Then an idea sprang to mind, one that would change my life. If gnomes indeed existed in the garden just beyond my front door, I would write them a letter and see if they replied! So out came a tiny piece of paper and a pencil so small that I had trouble holding it, and I unleashed my imagination onto the page. The words splashed themselves with wild abandon across the itsy bit of paper that I had to press down with my little finger:

"Dear Gnomes,

If you are out there, please write back. I will leave a pencil and some space at the bottom of this letter so you can do so. I would love to hear from you!

Love from Lani (the girl who lives in the house) xxx"

I confided my special secret in no one. Before I went to bed that night, and under the cover of the dark dusk sky, I placed the note at the front door, jutting out from under the doormat, hoping it would be seen by the gnomes but unseen and undisturbed by anyone else.

I remember feeling so excited when I went to bed that night; it took me a while to get to sleep from the excitement. When I awoke the next morning, before anyone else was awake, I bounded out of bed and went straight to the doormat to check the note. I couldn't believe my eyes! Sure enough, there was a reply in the tiniest writing I had ever seen! My wish had been fulfilled, like magic! The gnome must've been nervous, or worried about being caught, because the words had a shaky appearance.

I was so excited I picked up the note with fumbling hands and read the miniscule words. The gnome's name was Alex, he was 36 years old (gnomes don't mature until they're around 40, and their lives can span across three centuries!) and he was only a few centimetres tall. He had a pet rabbit (who was much larger than he was), he ate grass seeds and bugs and other garden delights, and had regular feasts, gatherings and celebrations with the other forest folk. I soon learned that gnomes are an intelligent race with an innate curiosity, charm, cheekiness, and an affinity for all things magical, especially the arcane. Alex was all this and more, and we became firm friends, exchanging around thirty notes over the next few months. Mostly, I only left letters out about once a week; Alex was a busy little young man and he said he couldn't reply all the time, as he took 'short' trips through the extensive bush and across the creek at the foot of our property, trips which often took him days, considering how small he was.

I asked various other questions and left spaces for him to answer. He told me about his hobbies, his many forest friends, his adventures, and even what possessions he had. Nevertheless, over time I became more curious, and asked him ever more personal and probing questions. I finally felt brave enough to ask him where he lived! I promised him that if he divulged this; I would not come looking for him, that I was simply wondering out of mere interest. This was one question he avoided answering directly, however. Instead, he answered my query as best he could without giving too much away.

Then one day our friendship came to an abrupt end. He left me a note under the doormat as always, but this time it wasn't all about fun and sharing. He informed me that he had an ill relative in a far-off place, and had to journey through bush, fields, tracks, and rivers to reach this place - he said he might even be gone forever, as gnomes sometimes had to move on if they found a new home elsewhere. He told me that if he wasn't back within say, a month, then it was likely that he wasn't coming back to our garden.

I accepted this news with surprising ease. It was fine with me, as I had enjoyed our friendship for its relatively short duration, and Alex had watered my imagination with enough magic to last me a lifetime. He had served his purpose and now it was time for him - and me - to move on. Instinctively, I understood this and wrote him one last note to say goodbye and thank you … but the reply I had hoped for never came.

Alex had gone, I thought momentarily woefully, swallowed by the foggy purple-hued dawn, misty forests, probably skipping somewhere playfully across the logs and rocks of swollen creeks, whistling a little gnome-inspired tune as he went, off to explore his new horizons. The thought ultimately made me happy; I was glad for him. Because deep down, I knew that our friendship had somehow touched and enriched his life also.

I don't remember how long it was after Alex's departure that I found out who the real writer of the letters was. I don't even remember *how* I found out. However, I found out anyway. At first, I was a little bit upset, because the enchanted exchanges I'd had with Alex somehow lost a bit of their glitter ... but then I realised how valuable the whole experience was - in essence, it was a writing journey that helped heal both myself, and the writer himself - *my Dad*!

It turned out that my dad, who was very sick, had been visiting friends on those nights that I left notes jutting out from under the doormat, and he often arrived home in the dark of night to find them under his feet as he unlocked the door. He always sat down and answered them straight away, and delighted in replying to my questions, which had become greater in number and detail. The reason he stopped, he told me in later years, was because my queries were becoming ever more complex and investigative, and his research into the world of gnomes could only stretch so far! (Remember these were the days before the internet). So he made up a little story that Alex had to leave the area and probably wouldn't be back - a perfect excuse to end the friendship on a nice, pleasant, clean-cut note.

I can only assume, but I am sure my dad healed through this writing journey - not only was he fostering my imagination and curiosity, he was also learning a lot himself - about gnomes (my book was dog-earmarked in many places!), but mostly about the power of his own imagination, essence, higher mind faculties and long-neglected creativity. It even had the added benefit of taking his mind off his condition and inevitable fate for those short moments in the dark silence of the nights as he immersed himself in writing.

I went on to writing creative fictional pieces and little chapter books, mostly centering around fantasy creatures such as fairies, elves, pixies, and of course gnomes. I even believed all of them actually existed until I was at least eleven years old.

My dad Graham died when he was just 43 years old, one August afternoon in 1989, a substantial 16 years after the initial diagnosis, which had informed him he only had months to live! He defied the medical professionals and lived much longer than this prognosis anticipated he would.

I feel lucky that we got so much extra time with my father, and blessed that I had such a magical, spellbinding presence in my life. In essence, my dad taught me so much, which could indeed fill a whole book … but not nearly as much as Alex did …

HEALING THE WRITE WAY

By Karen McDermott

We will all face challenges throughout our lives. That's how we grow in maturity and spirit. How we choose to react and embrace those challenges can often depend on where we are in life when we experience them. If we are already vulnerable it may knock us lower, if we are flying high we may not learn from the occurrence and may have to experience the life lesson again sometime in our future, if we are living a positive, loving life we will usually embrace the trauma, sadness or incident from a loving, life learning perspective and through honouring our suffering we will find a way to heal and maybe even the desire in turn help others.

When we endure a dark time, it may feel like the end of our world, and in one way, it is as it can often spell the end of a way we once became accustomed to. But it is important to note the life altering opportunity to reinvent and embrace a renewed vision for ourselves of how we would like to move forward. If we have the courage and open mindedness to embrace it, wonderful things can happen.

The true emotions and lessons that come to the surface can only really be felt when a challenge has been endured and through others experiences we can find hope and the strength to carry on. It is at this point when writing about the journey is the most powerful healer. Intention is set and not only will the writer heal themselves in the process they will touch and heal the heart of someone at a time of much need. It is like a healing eclipse where the overlap shines bright and powerful throughout the world producing electric energy that can create opportunities for people to heal themselves through hope.

When I introduced writing into my life everything seemed to make more sense, I could articulate my journey better and create a deeper understanding for myself along the way. I also seem to learn more about life and myself as I write and this enables me to grow in many ways. I am not what you may expect to be a normal stereotype for being a writer but that does not stop me. The more I write the more I grow as a writer. I started small and grew from then.

Firstly, I began writing articles of interest and about my journey. I couldn't stop writing these once I started and before long I had over fifty written and published. They then began to be picked up by the Universal Mind magazine and so I knew that I must have been doing something right. I have never written for glory; I write because it makes me feel wonderful to open my heart and let it all flow out. I have had three fictional novels published, fifteen children's books and including this piece; I have had three short biographical stories published. As you can see, I do not restrict myself to any specific genre because through all genres you can heal. My first fictional novel was the most healing piece I have ever written, I think that this was because it allowed me more freedom to express and expand the reality so I didn't feel like I needed to keep anything hidden or protect identities.

We all have different things that happen to us during our lives that we need to heal from. Here is a short piece about some of life's challenges that I needed to recover from:

In December 2007, I endured a miscarriage. It was lengthy and as I was already at a low point in my life, it affected me deeply. This was not the reaction I expected to have as we were not trying for a baby but when we discovered we were expecting it had put some much needed magic back into our lives and I so didn't want to let it go, I wanted this baby so much. I don't ever remember praying so hard in all of my life but after two long weeks, trips to the hospital and lying trying desperately to save it the inevitable happened. I couldn't stop crying, I cannot recall crying so hard ever before during my life. Floods of tears streamed my face and every night I felt so empty and I prayed so hard to be full again. Deep down I knew that the tears flowing were not only just for the little angel I lost they were also for the old me that had become lost too. A year or so previous I had endured an incident that shook me to my core. I suffered from post-traumatic stress disorder during this time. Unless you have experienced it, you will never know what it is like but I will try to explain it to you.

Firstly, there was an instant shadow that covered my mind; everything around me seemed instantly duller. I was so tense and went into a mode that I call 'survival mode', which is when you just do what is needed to get by. I experienced a tunnel vision whereas everything in my peripheral vision was dark and I was only focused on what was in front of me. The most poignant thing was that I had an overwhelming feeling that something had shifted and things were never going to be the same again. This feeling is very unsettling and looking back now I think that the shock of that alone was very the thing that had the most impact on me. Everything that I was striving towards achieving didn't seem so important anymore. I had to accept that things were going to be different and no matter how hard I would push to make that not be the case it wouldn't change it. I felt defeated in a way and for a high achiever that I was proud to call myself beforehand that was a very shocking realisation.

Luckily, I had worked for almost four years in a mental health setting and was aware of mental vulnerabilities. I had never studied it but I was aware that what I needed to do was to not be fearful of what was happening to me and to be gentle on myself. I knew that there was not going to be any successful quick fix and that I was going to have to take time out to heal. I know that I withdrew from my family during this time and I know that I was no longer the feisty go getter that I had always been, but that is what I needed to do at this time and so I went with it. I slowed down and I went inward. If something felt right I did it, if it didn't I didn't. I wasn't the caring considerate person I had been beforehand who would have given anything she had to make someone else happy, no, I needed to focus on myself and I needed all of the love I had within me to keep for loving and healing myself. The only exceptions were my two boys and then my partner.

One day I remember visiting my old boss from the mental health day care centre that I had worked at for almost four years; she was always so open and caring and someone that I could really trust. I remember chatting to her and let some things flow that I had been keeping inside. I began to shake uncontrollably when I spoke about certain things and she asked in the most gentlest way "Karen you do know that you are suffering from post-traumatic stress?" and I of course responded with a "Yes I did think that, but I have to deal with it my way and get myself through it the best that I can and I am". She was satisfied with my intentions and did not pursue it further. I knew that if I ever needed her she was there and that was comforting to know and that slight release was good for me, it felt as though I had let a little of the poison out.

It carried on and carried on and I have to say that I never felt happy or joyful whilst going through the motions. In fact I found it hard to smile or laugh, this was totally out of character for me as I had always been a happy person; the 'Bridget Jones' of our family~ tragic and unpredictable but fun to be around. I do not know what others thought of my transformation but the difference must have seemed immense to them. I found it hard to commit to choices but the bizarre thing was that I did make one huge decision during this time and that was to apply for a visa to move to Australia. This would never have been even a consideration beforehand but it felt right and I felt as though I was doing it for my family and myself so I went with it.

About a year passed and that is when I discovered I was expecting. It was a glimmer of hope and suddenly I was smiling again. Then to begin losing the pregnancy a week later, I was totally distraught. This was going to make things better; I wanted it so much. There was a shining light though as amazingly I fell pregnant again the next month and to this day I really don't know how it happened but in my heart I knew that I was gifted something very special and I embraced it with an open heart. I discovered that once I had opened my heart to this the darkness that had been shadowing all aspects of my life for a time began to fade away and light began to flow back in. Wonderful things started to happen and I was feeling purpose and love again. I was becoming happy again, a light that had been dimmed was radiating from my inner core once again and I knew at this moment that the pain I had endured was for my greater good. I felt more fulfilled and ready to move forward in excitement. I had a wonderful feeling that I had finally shifted from the darkness back into the light.

2008 was a big year for me as I got married in May, immigrated to Australia in September with my husband and two boys and had my gorgeous girl in October. However, I never forgot the little gem that I lost; it stayed in my heart and close to my every thought for some time. It had brought me the opportunity to live again, gave me a wakeup call and shifted me back onto the right track, it had given gave me a light to follow through the darkness. I was so grateful. I began feeling an urge to write.

I was never good at English at school but had later gone back to complete a Diploma in Humanities. At the time, I did not know why I chose the course but now I did. I began experiencing huge realisations and had many epiphany moments. Then when signs started flowing from other real life sources like beacons I knew that I had to take my interest seriously. I began writing short articles for www.buildingbeautifulbonds.com about my journey and things that interested me. This opened up the floodgates and before I knew, I had signed up for a novel writing month.

Again, affirmations where all around me letting me know that I was on the right path. For that month I wrote and wrote 1667 words every day consistently and at the end of it I had my first novel 'The Visitor~ a magical understanding of uncertainty'. This novel has had a profound impact on my life and on the people it finds. I know that this is because it was written through my heart. I know the energy I channelled when I was writing was projected onto every page and the readers when they came across it. When someone reads it, who is also on their own spiritual journey the connection is very magical. I healed as I wrote it and I truly believe that my readers can connect directly with that powerful healing energy. Even though it is a work of fiction my own personal story is weaved through it and it shows that you can write about true events and it doesn't have to be biographical this can assist with people who have reservations about writing their story because they don't feel comfortable sharing it with the world or don't want the sharing of their story impact on their loved ones.

I have discovered many things about writing, especially from my own experiences. It is very therapeutic in helping put things in perspective when you may feel lost or confused. When you write something down you are making it a tangible thing. It is out of your head where it can be confusing and overwhelming and now it is something real, something to face, something to look at from a different perspective. It has been released! It makes it easier to find a solution, see how far you have come or even help someone else.

There are many ways that this can be achieved:

Through poetry: Poetry is filled with emotion. It can be harmonious or gritty. It is filled with a poetic rhythm that is a gift from the poet to their readers.

Through fiction: Fiction is great as it allows you more freedom to be honest and explore avenues that may not have actually occurred.

Through blogging: Blogging is an instant way of reaching readers, building up a following and connecting with others instantly.

Through a biographical story: Being more personal and in-depth about your life can directly help others through tough times, especially when they are written from a positive, loving and solution based perspective. If your intention is to share your story to help others then this will come through in your writing. Even though we all will experience our own personal challenges that will not be exactly the same as someone else's, we all have the ability to connect with someone through our words.

Through keeping a journal: Journaling has always been a popular way to share thoughts and emotions. They are renowned for being private and anyone who violates the unspoken rule of diary snooping will bear the consequences of possibly reading something about themselves or learning something about the author that they may not like. They often harbour secrets and the reason for this is because secrets that are kept within can be damaging on our emotional wellbeing and physical health so sharing the secret by writing it to a non-judgemental source like a diary you may feel that it is not so much a secret anymore.

Writing is a huge part of my life now. It makes me happy and I know that I will forever embrace the magic of words. I am proud to say that I live a fully creative life. It takes courage to do this but the rewards are amazing and life changing. Yes, I do feel fear of sharing my writing sometimes and I honour that fear by acknowledging it but I know deep down that I share my thoughts and words with the intention of helping others and myself so that we can heal and grow together. It has opened up so many avenues in life for me personally. I now own my own publishing company called Serenity Press, I love compiling collections of inspiring stories that help people find hope. I am able to publish my own work and maintain the rights to my own work and I am able to help people get self-published in a positive and more economical way. I also get to work closely with community groups to publish their projects; this is very fulfilling for me. I am very grateful for all of the blessings I have received and those that I can give to others.

The learning potential from writing is endless and healing potential is also endless. I no longer feel that I am keeping things in. I release everything and that allows me to heal and move forward at a very steady pace. I have also discovered that as I write I find that I tend to think things through more clearly and find amicable solutions from a wider perspective. Happiness helps us to heal; physically we release happy hormones that are actually good for us. This happiness ripple effects those closest to us at this time and that can only be a good thing. Those closest to us should be happy that we are happy, if you find that they are not that is fine they are not yet ready to understand but don't let that stop you, find a way to make it work for you because it is important.

I have discovered that when the right words find the right person at the right time magic happens in their life. They may go through a shift, one that may unsettle them for a time or one that they may find the answer they had been hoping for through reading them. Whatever the outcome the words have touched that person in a deep and influential way gifting them the opportunity to make a positive change in their life if they find the courage to follow it through. Then consequently, their transforming perspective will in turn affect the lives of those that surround them and so on…..The healing potential is huge and very powerful and that is why I feel that words written with the intention of inspiring others are so important.

It is important to remember that if we focus on the negatives in life our experience and perspective of life will be negative. If you focus on the positives in life, your experience and perspective will be a positive one. It is that simple and yet we, as humans, tend to over complicate things; it is just in our nature to do so.

Thank you for taking the time to read my story. I have attached some of my articles that I feel may be helpful when reading about Writing being the powerful healer. I wish you the best of luck on your journey.

POETRY

By Ella Kate Reeves

My name is Ella Kate Reeves. I am and dance and movement therapist, psychotherapist an award-winning poet, an internationally published. I have performed throughout the Sussex and London area and fused projects with other artists.

I hold degrees in Media Studies and Cultural Studies and specialised in Shamanic consciousness and post-feminist sexual politics. I am also am a certified and accredited teacher/psychotherapist. I live in the UK , near Brighton ,with my husband , and son Louis.

Poetry has been a vehicle for me to express that which I find difficult to express in conversation or prose. My style is visceral, rhythmic and raw. I also really enjoy 'ecopoetry' and write for a couple of publishing companies. Writing is a fundamental part of my life now and I relate to it as medicine for the soul! My book 'Watering my soul', started after I had brain surgery, to remove a tumour. I wrote from my hospital bed daily (and sometimes all night!).

I now continue to write, and am starting to run wild poetry workshops; combining walks in nature, dance, yoga and poetry.

Stripped it all away

A shining seven year old dancing star

Sparkling, smiling, bursting with life

A sweet cocktail of energy and innocence

... You were thirsty and desperate

And I didn't see it coming...

Young entertainer of the year, gold

Yes I felt golden for that moment, I didn't believe the speech you gave

She sounded magical, she sounded perfect

That was the last gift you gave me

Before you stripped it all away.

The spotlight scared me and I froze

You scooped me up and the curtain went down

'you're gonna be a star' he whispers before he kisses me on the lips

And shoves his tongue down my throat

I bite hard and he drops me

But I knew no one was around

And you stripped what was left away.

Storing that story away i carry on full of shame

But my body feels different, blocked

I start to crave sugar and hate myself

Food becomes a refuge, my comfort blanket against the world

So I dive under the duvet and stay there

Hiding, denying, numbing what he'd stripped away.

I'm sixteen now and this guy appears

He's intense and clever and fascinated with me

' I won't tell you I love you so that I can fuck you' ,he confesses one night.

I'm hurt but can't summon the courage to ask him to leave.

So we carry on as if somehow it's ok

And I fall into what I thought was love with him

What I thought was love

He breaks me open and after a year I let go

We get close and he's become my world

And I've become his

Inseparable we get the Romeo Juliet status

And then I realise that if I don't get out I will be in prison

So I end it

End what I thought was love.

He won't let go and loses the plot

I can't stand the guilt and numb out

Then he finds me one night and takes what's 'his'

He strips what's left of me away.

As he leaves me, he reminds me that he was my first

'you'll never forget me because I took your innocence'

As I lie there bleeding I shout, ' you haven't taken anything!'

But I knew he had, I felt ripped and stripped away.

I'm a little older now and know there are no victims, no villains

This time he's a French Lord

Prince and princess

Bastard and bitch

Wizard and witch

No one's gonna strip me away.

Were good lovers for years

But there's this divine delicate line

Between playing with our energy and crossing the line

But he does and I know

that in time, he will strip it all away.

Patchwork Majesty

Tick tock

the linear clock

has finally stopped.

All that strife and life

flowing throw these veins-

tick tock, I've stopped....

They could not bring my body back.

And they tried so diligently

Did this and that.

But I soared about my soul

And nothing drew me back.

I knew I was going

Four minutes dead, so they say.

But they could not know

I was here in every way !

Four minutes dead

-so much more on a cosmic clock.
Began to tick so loudly,
how could I make it stop?
With all physical cords cut,
I began to be
inside a new world,
Panoramic 6D.
I knew now my life
thus far had been
repressed, unravelled, ecstatic, extreme.
I saw my life played back
-and what a shock to see
I'd missed the best view

-in search of ecstasy!
I'd followed the path

of 'liberation and celebration'.
Thought that's what it was all about?
So how come right here, right now

I'm in such deep isolation?

As I reach out to

the souls I'd truly loved

who'd passed , I hoped they'd guide me home,

maybe even help me cross?

But that didn't happen-

Instead a voice came forth;

'If it's not about freedom, ecstasy, liberation'-I asked

'then what the fuck has my life been serving?'

'IT"S VERY SIMPLE', I heard.

This voice that's not mine, how fucking absurd?

'IT"S JUST ABOUT KINDNESS AND COMPASSION'

I'm still, I'm empty.

Too late now, I got it so wrong-

I let go into death and say my final farewell;

'Rob and Mum please take care of my son'.

Then the voice returns and says;

'NO, IT'S YOU HE NEEDS. LATER YOU WILL SEE'

An electrical impulse

surges through my soul.

Im suddenly conscious,

so awake

And knowing what to tell the doctors to take!

'Blood from my left toe!'

My veins had collapsed.

'But there's usually one in your left toe,-please try!'

So the team take blood

and chaos begins.

They bring me

BACK TO LIFE.

BUT I've crossed over-

the bridge and seen the view.

My souls returned anew.

And life's never been the same....

Veiled

Can't you see?
The cracks
in my walls
the crumbling wreck
and ruins that lead me
to these edges
time and time again
The deeper I dive
the higher I fall-
-and as I stare down
at the view
I tremble and shake
and have to remind
myself of
the promise
I made
to never play safe.
Or live an unlived life

and the life I chose
is not on my terms....
Thy will not mine be done.

Can't you see?
The slashes
of swords
and scattered scar tissue
-stitches and slits
holding this body together
housing the sacred city
of this soul
it's not young or old
shy nor bold-
You see you do not see
the soreness and tears
the holding and fears
that ripple through
these veins

and choke all my maternal reins
of the raw bitter sweet silk
I'm weaving for mother nature someday.
Thy will not mine be done.

Can't you see?
I hold myself tight
and ground down
into roots of the earth
So that I'm able to
sprout out to the heavens
and cry out
'I DO NOT KNOW IF I CAN LIVE IN THIS WORLD'
Fuck it's not fair!
My babies crumbling wings
and twisting skin
cut me up
and shut me in
this tiny room

and behind these curtains lies

an endless roar of agony...

Thy will not mine be done.

I'm not just writing

I'm not just writing

I'm unearthing creatures

inside I tried to hide and couldn't

ancestral knots -

hangovers from centuries ago

I'm not just writing

I'm unravelling my

soul strung mojo

yeah,- I need to reach deep in there

and there to

fish out the crap

that's trapped

and stale-the calcified fear

all that loneliness

that got stuck in the web

way, way back.

I'm not just writing
I'm reclaiming the witch and crone
Shedding down to bone
Climbing out of the closet
and redefining, refining
new skins and tails
striking a cord in
the spaces and gaps
displaced by the confused parts
that got abused, raped.
I'm not just writing
I'm dancing into myself
time and time again
setting myself on fire
and free

I'm not just writing
I'm showing all of me.

Releasing Machisma

Your hands have slid down too far

this body was never

an open invitation to take .

You are a crazy unknown force

Drunk on emptiness that I will never fill.

A thick black sludge penetrates my skin.

You have crossed over into me

Without consent.

No one is here.

So you will keep taking

I ache for Mother earth to save me….

But she's ignored

As is my request to stop.

Taken advantage of-

Her riches mined for all

they are worth.

Human-unkinds greed and arrogance,

desecrates,

dirties

and

defiles.

Her, and my body.

Does he not feel our interconnectedness?

Does he feel anything besides me?

When will we learn?

We are stripping the feminine away.

Past the point of return

We are wounding the nutrients

and lush forests of our hearts?

We can no longer ignore

We are the trees sea and earth

Can we make her safe again?

She holds the key.

And despite his attempt to access and open her.

He can't.

And he knows she won't permit access!

This is not what I asked for or wanted.

This is your desire and rape.

And as I stare into those

empty , aroused eyes.

I have no doubt I will get out.

And I do.

But he has crossed my line.

Attempted to thieve something divine.

Golden-power, and it's MINE.

So as I run and shake-

-I vomit him out

and out

and

out.

And take this body into the sea.

Cleanse myself and remember/

This soul is free.

But he would have polluted this environment far more….

And this energy must stop.

So much 'she' has been made 'he'.

She has had to take on 'he' to access power

In this strange world.

Where he takes and takes

While 'she' is the very force-

that can redress this corruption!

She can bring us out of the darkness

Put the wild hunger where it really belongs

Within the act of creation,

Crude power that forges a balance.

Help us out of this state

Without light nothing flowers .

No more stripping away.

No more.

No

I said no.

And I mean it.

The Naked in All

In a gentle world, across the gulf of time.

I take off all my clothes , let my hair blow free.

The flowers dont mind and the sea invites me in.

Into a sea of nevereverlessness.

So I bathe, and ride the waves beyond time.

My naked truth sits in my womb - stream.

Still , sublime.

I trust this soul spot inside at my base;

It's guidance, holding, power and grace.

To blossom me out and open my wings.

My roots run deep and my wings are strong.

My heart is the place where

ALL PATHS MEET.

ALL PATHS MEET IN MY ROOTS OF MY HEART.

I am the dancing universe, I am one with all.

I am divine untamed female energy ,but what's more;

I am extraordinarily ordinary

I am the naked truth in all.

Practising for what?

Funny how we 'practice',
'spiritual paths'?
Get tied in knots
idea's ,ideals
and fixed beliefs!
All that orthodox crap
Those toxic hippycritts
and flakey drips.
The 'trusterferians'
Floating broken- hearted souls
Raw food airians.

Where's the breath
being received
In the darkest hour?
The painless seat

in the tightest knot
The crux of asana.
Bored of acrobats
and ego-battles.
Wrapped in spiritual frills
All the cloaked sticky mantra's....

Practising for what I ask?
It's the one's you cross
when the soul runs dry .
The one's you meet
in the roughest storms.
The souls that
guide you back
to your deepest dream.

The alchemist in you
needs reminding-
to displace 'the victim'

of your story
grace your own system.
So don't fall victim
to a toxic rhythm!

To stand at the feet of your life
and use everything as fuel-
Lessons are blessings
blessings are lessons
and let your heart break.
The HEART can filter anything
that the alchemist embraces
and if you are awake
the heart will
break and break...

See more of Ella's work at

www.wateringmysoul.wix.com/ellakatereeves

WRITE IT OUT...IT REALLY WORKS!

By Jessie Welsh

The thought of writing about my life scared the hell out of me! I spent many nights awake weighing up my options and wondering whether it would work or be worth it. After some serious thought and questioning why I was so concerned about it, I came to a conclusion. It wasn't that I was concerned about laying my soul bare (which I don't do easily); the truth is, I was concerned about going back to the places I thought I had left behind. I had only been fooling myself. You see, at this point in my life I was 'lost'. I was looking for meaning. I had begun my spiritual journey full time and I realised that I couldn't be walking around anymore with these 'demons' on my shoulder.

Once I finally sat down at the computer and began typing my detailed account of my life to that point, I began to feel lighter. What I realised I was doing was removing the weight of the world that I felt was weighing down my spirit. I didn't get it all done in one night. I wanted it to be detailed, and make sure that I really expressed the emotion that I felt but also, as I was typing more and more things would come to mind that I had forgotten about or subconsciously locked away. I guess we do this as a form of self-preservation, but is that what it really does? I don't think so. It just weighs down the shelf which eventually has to crumble under the pressure.

What I discovered was incredibly important to my life's journey. I was now able to gain clarity. I was able to look at my experiences from a new perspective and I had a more mature mindset to do so too. Because of the distance I had gained from these past experiences; both good and bad, I was able to replay what had happened, look at my emotions and reactions, see the reasoning behind it as a whole and let it go. Now, don't get me wrong, I certainly haven't erased it all from my life, but I have lessened the effect and hold that it once had on me. Our experiences will never totally go away, and that's important because they are what make us who we are. They serve a purpose whether a pleasant experience or not, and shape us into the beings we are today.

If someone asked me where I would be today had I not written my story, I would definitely be able to say not where I am now, pretty obvious right? However, I honestly can't tell you where I would be because I don't know and I wasn't giving myself the time to find out either. I needed to express my past hurts, my past joys and really allow myself to process and come to terms with all that I've experienced. I'm one of those people who finds it not only hard to articulate to others how I'm feeling, but just honestly expressing my true feelings too. There is a part of me that needs to keep my emotions and feeling to myself and this often frustrates me. It's not that I don't want to, it's just there is something vulnerable about it that makes me uncomfortable so I don't do it very often. I need to be able to roll the experience and emotions around my own head and internalise the entire thing before I will even contemplate opening up and going outward with it, and sometimes, I don't mention anything to anyone.

This is where writing is incredibly important (and lifesaving), not only for me but for others, especially since I can bottle and eventually explode. I mention this because if you too are like me and don't readily express your emotions for whatever reason, please try writing them instead. You can keep it to yourself or you can show others; that's entirely up to you, but the act alone of just writing about them is really quite liberating.

So, do I feel that writing is a valuable and healing tool? Absolutely! It is something that I recommend often throughout my work and to my students, because I know first-hand that it can and will make a difference to that little demon on your shoulder, who feels like the weight of the world.

RIGHT TO HEAL

By Shauna Norman

Quite a few years ago whilst working in a Community Welfare position at a local neighbourhood centre, I became aware of a climate of favouritism and bullying from the upper management. This behaviour, I began to notice was also imitated by the regular staff. As time went on, I watched and took notes; I spoke out, fortunately I protected myself by joining the union and I continued to work my butt off in a place that had no idea of ethics, clinical supervision and duty of care or even professional liability.

My colleague, a youth/IT Worker, was enduring one of many rounds of chemotherapy for bowel cancer and had the added discomfort of small metal rods in both of her wrists, which were inserted as a part of her treatment after she suffered a serious fall. She was the target of this bullying campaign and as a result was treated like a packhorse; expected to cart the carry bags of grocery items for welfare recipients and boxes of office supplies that a healthy woman would have had trouble with. She was snickered at, backstabbed, ridiculed, ignored and ostracised by the workplace clique. I must add, at the time, most of the staff employed at the centre were neither qualified nor trained in the positions they were employed or paid for.

I was the latest recruit and the flavour of the month and as such it didn't take long for members of the staff to attempt to lure me into the pack. There were dinner invites, lunches together in the staff room, gift giving, and over-obliging offers of assistance. Along with this came a continuum of malicious stories against the youth/IT worker and the social worker before me.

As time went on, I soon found myself working back-to-back suicide cases and often went home without having been debriefed. I was trying to fit an extra six hours into a normal working day and eventually the inevitable happened; one of the inexperienced girls on staff knocked on my door and asked if I could see a young man who appeared very anxious. There was no way I could make room for him in the midst of the busy schedule I already had.

However, I did make time to speak with him briefly between clients. I gave him an emergency phone number for a man in the Alcoholics Anonymous (AA) fellowship as he was in early recovery from Alcoholism and was afraid of relapsing. I knew the man whose number I gave him would go out of his way for vulnerable alcoholics. I told my potential client where there was a meeting that afternoon and made him an appointment for later in the week. As he was leaving, he assured me he was going to the meeting and that he was also going to ring the number I had given him.

A gnawing feeling rode around with me like an unwanted hitchhiker for several days and in the end I rang the caravan park that was on the clients file card. I was unceremoniously informed that the young man had been found dead in his caravan. He had relapsed and then committed suicide. I took this tragedy home with me with the same regularity as I took my handbag. I blamed myself for what I perceived as my having dropped the ball, even though now after much professional help, I know it was out of my hands – I had been powerless.

Even when I wasn't at work, staff continuously rang me with questions relating to a walk-in client, my diary, or blatant attempts to gossip about other staff members. Where they weren't able to ally me, they did manage to secure the allegiance of the head of the management committee.

Between the unprofessional running of the centre and my workload, my health was going downhill fast; I was in a constant state of anxiety and began suffering chest pains and other debilitating symptoms. One day the pains were so severe that when, at my son's insistence, I finally rang the doctor's surgery, I was instructed to come straight in. After a quick assessment, the GP called an ambulance and I was rushed off to the ER at John Hunter Hospital, where a suspected heart attack was diagnosed as a panic attack, which later became panic disorder.

There was no one in the workplace I could turn to. I had begun formulating a report concerning the bullying of my co-worker and the many other unethical practices I had either witnessed or was told about by staff members who later hid behind the skirts of upper-level management – for fear of losing their own jobs. The youth /IT Worker was, by this time, too sick to work and was off on leave.

The time came when I had no ethical choice but to submit my report to the management committee. The manager was one of the worst offenders in the litany of complaints I had formulated and her band of merry helpers ran around after her like fan wavers chasing pharaohs. As such, I soon found myself the recipient of a vendetta of in-house abuse I did not dream possible. I was banned from my own office unless I had a client, and my reports and case notes were to be written up in the lunch room or in the client waiting room. No personal items were to be displayed in my office, my projects were shut down – including a newly opened soup kitchen, my hours decreased from thirty-six to six, within days of my complaint being received, and the management committee was nowhere to be seen. The chairwoman was rarely visible; it seemed the more the centre fell into crisis, the less we saw of her, although she did manage to find time to send trivial emails unrelated to work, to some staff members.

I had ironically managed to obtain a very professional clinical supervisor who, having been very versed on the in-house mismanagement of the centre and the breaches in policy and procedure, vehemently advised me to get my personal belongings and get my butt out of there, STAT!!!

No one mentioned breakdown. Actually looking back, I can't remember when I was informed or how I ended up knowing... I just remember I knew I had never felt anything so physically emotional before, and that was minor compared to how I felt/ or didn't feel, mentally. I cried a lot, I hardly slept, my chest ached constantly, I was medicated and it was continually increased. It wasn't long before depression joined the now diagnosed anxiety and panic disorders - I had the trifecta. The day came when I could do it no more; I went into work, but only managed to stay long enough to clear out my desk.

I consistently felt shame and humiliation; going down to the local shopping centre filled me with fear and dread; if I saw someone I knew, I felt embarrassed and eventually relied on my daughter more and more to take care of tasks outside the home.

Suddenly, I was being shuffled between a mass of men and women from within the professional world: lawyers, psychologists, psychiatrists, doctors, even dentists (they don't warn you that a combination of medication and jaw clenching is not good for your teeth). Appointments were made all over the countryside; Newcastle, the Central Coast, and as far as Macquarie St Sydney. Some even came to the house 'for my convenience', to assess the legitimacy of my deteriorating health.

Finally, Workcover ruled I had suffered a psychological injury caused by workplace bullying. I was placed on a disability support pension and left to my own devices. Had I not taken ownership of my own health, I dread to think where I might be today. Having said that, I would be neglect if I did not add, I am still not well today, but some of this has been exacerbated by incidences unrelated to the workplace.

Where does my writing come into this? I was already qualified in creative writing and was online regularly, when I experienced a setback two years later. Being mentally and emotionally fragile, I was not equipped to cope with another challenge and knew the symptoms only too well the next time it happened.

I made a decision; not one of my best, but a decision just the same, to sell, give away or throw out most of my belongings, and place the remainder in storage while I basically couch surfed for several months. Having just turned fifty, this would have already been questionable, having doubtful mental health, my decision left many people scratching their heads. However, tagging it with the word 'adventure' took some of the doubt and concern away for most of them.

I was an active member of Facebook and as the word got around, friends started saying they wanted to come with me. I shared these comments with my son and added, "How silly, they can't come with me; they live all over the world". He assured me that they in fact could; he would build me a blog and they could travel around with me that way, and that is exactly what happened.

Every day, rain, hail or shine, I posted on that blog, I had a task - something I could focus on. I posted no matter how bad I felt; I posted it all. I included pictures and as time went on, I also added a combination of three or more of the following: 'My Learning for Today', 'My Prayer or Blessing for Today', 'Gratitude for Today', a 'Quote for Today', a 'Hint for Today' and almost always, 'My Favourite Book for Today'. The blog was in very raw form, with lots of typos, spelling and grammatical errors, but it was free flowing and I posted it the way it came out.

In taking up this daily challenge, I was obliged to do something. I had at least one thing I was responsible for and even some people whom I felt I was responsible to. Some days it took me hours, while other days, I could throw something together in no time at all. What often kept me focused were the comments, and even though they were mostly posted on my Facebook page - where I loaded my blog at the end of each day, they encouraged me to stay true to myself and to get well.

At the time, it was also a bit of a cumbersome exercise; there were no iPads or smaller devices like there are today, so I would lug my trusty old laptop around... literally, on trains, aeroplanes, even a big old rust bucket four-wheel drive. It was there that I sat squashed up in the back amongst all form of farm equipment and hoarder's delights... but I wrote, and I wrote and I wrote.

I had one of those little gadgets you stick in the front of your laptop and it connects you to the internet, so I was able to upload, or is it download? I always confuse my loads...anyway, I would get it posted from somewhere. I recall sitting in the airport in Melbourne and noticed my power was running out... so I just wandered aimlessly around with my luggage on one of those odd, heavy trolleys, until I saw a random power point, then I nonchalantly set myself down near it, plugged in and away I went.

When I remember this period in my life, I can usually counteract a bad experience with a positive one. For example, I had three cats: Cindee, Winnie and Pooh. It had torn my heart apart having to separate from them, but at the eleventh hour I had them homed with good people, for indefinite periods. Cindee was with a friend and the twins were with a couple I had never met, but who had read my desperate ad on the internet begging someone to give me any alternative to save them from going to a shelter where workers had all but told me, they would not get adopted (we know what that means, don't we?) Warren and Cherie contacted me and told me not only would they foster them but they would do so until I was well enough to take them back. "I would get them back?" I thought. I was beside myself with relief. During the six month separation, we kept in touch on Facebook; they read my blog and posted photographs of them for me. So again, because of my writing and a couple of lovely strangers (who are still my friends) my healing was assisted.

It was only a year after this, and settling in a small rural community, I lost my grandson. This was a heartbreaking tragedy for all of us - one that takes a lot of getting over. Again, I ran - this time to Grafton and then Port Macquarie - and lived out of suitcases for another six months after putting my life into a storage container.

One of the places I stayed, I was expected to look after the woman's grandchildren and at times, her friends' three children as well, do her housework, and clean up her filthy yard. Never had I seen such a hoarded mess of dog bones, car parts, garden vegetation and household waste all in the one place. In addition to all of this, I was also expected to house sit while she went to Sydney and then to Queensland and put up with her racist comments about the local Indigenous people. Thankfully, I had a close girlfriend, Shanette who I had known all my life, living within walking distance, who pointed out to me just how much I was being used and abused. At the time, I was too sick to identify it for myself. I just knew my back ached day and night, my heart was shattered over the loss I was trying to deal with, and I was continually being left with other people's children and housework.

While in Grafton, I began writing during the night; it helped me tune out the continuous sound of raised voices, which reverberated around me. Before I walked out on a thirty-plus year friendship, I completed two short stories for an American publisher, who was putting together an anthology on phobias. A writer/editor on my Facebook page posted a submission notice for it and I thought, why not? It was an incredible experience for me. While writing about my fear of frogs, I was confronted with a load of ugly memories, however, reflecting on my experiences with escalators actually revealed lots of compassionate, yet surprisingly funny, interactions with both family members and total strangers.

Staying in Port Macquarie, after leaving Grafton, was a polar opposite experience to what I had just had. I was surrounded by Buddha's, young adults, laughter and gentleness. We spent our days talking, going to the beach and smelling the ocean, travelling the country roads on photography trips and simply hanging out. It was a soothing balm on very raw wounds. I continued to write.

Finally, I settled back in Newcastle where I am now and where I had previously loved living around twelve years ago. My heart had always remained here; I simply had to bring my body back to join it.

My writing came to a bit of a standstill for a period as I dealt with a new diagnosis of complex Post Traumatic Stress Disorder; of which I had been able to keep suppressed, or at least at bay, until the workplace bullying and the events which followed. Even though both my memory and my writing skills have been greatly affected by my illness/es, I am forever cultivating stories in my head - they will simply need to be professionally edited in future. This past year has seen me diligently click clacking away at all hours of the day and night, working hard on my current project: **"Hello, my name is Dollie"**, which is being published later this year.

You can find Shauna on FACEBOOK at Author Shauna Norman – where you can access her blog DISCOVERING DOLLIE.

You can order Phobias © 2014 published by Hidden Thoughts Press on Amazon.com – written by Shauna 'Fear Of Moving Steps and Family, Frogs and Phobias'.

Hello, my name is Dollie

'Hello, My Name is Dollie' is the true story of a woman 20 years sober in Alcoholics Anonymous. Where many books of this genre focus mainly on one person's life in and after addiction, this book differs in many ways. For one thing, Dollie's story includes mini-stories from women who have travelled the road of sobriety with her, either for many years or simply through some of the most recent steps. Between them all, they shine a light on many of the dark crevices where devious trolls hide waiting to lure them back into the pits of hell, or make sobriety one of the hardest battles they have ever had to face. These trolls come in the form of sexual predators, workplace bullies, mental illness, prostitution, rape and suicide, parenting and step parenting, switching the witch for the bitch. AA in contemporary Australia… and many others.

ARTICLES FROM OUR AUTHORS

Healing the write way

Karen McDermott

"People who engage in expressive writing report feeling happier and less negative than before writing. Similarly, reports of depressive symptoms, rumination, and general anxiety tend to drop in the weeks and months after writing about emotional upheavals."

James W. Pennebaker

Do you write? Whether it is in a diary, a blog, on a piece of scrap paper.

The one thing I have come to appreciate most over the past few years is the healing ability of writing things down. I have discovered that it is just as, if not more so, effective in getting thoughts out of our heads and shared. I am sure that you have heard of the saying 'A problem shared is a problem halved'. Well sometimes there may not be anyone there to share the problem with. We may feel that we don't want the problem to be resolved by another, we just need to release it.

My theory

Many of us good-natured souls have the inbuilt ability and desire to help others with their problems and often execute wonderful solutions to help someone through the most challenging of times. Wisdom can often ooze out of our pores for all to reap the benefits of when they are most in need and that is wonderful, but when it comes to ourselves and our own challenges we can't see things as clearly because it is shadowed by emotion.

When we take the time to write our concerns down we are making the problem a reality rather than a thought that can be hidden from sight and shadowed. It makes it real; it makes it something that we can approach from a different perspective and possible find the resolution to for ourselves. Writing can help us to heal.

Physical Health benefits

As you know, I have always been interested in metaphysics. How the energy we create through our thoughts and emotions can influence our lives is so fascinating to me. To know that we have the power and ability to control our energy frequencies is such an empowering prospect to me. Of course, the physics of the body and biology are sure to be linked. Louise Hay has shown us all how our thoughts and emotions can have physical impacts on our bodies, from a toothache right through to cancer and heart diseases. Her book and DVD 'Heal your Life' has opened so many people up to alternative ways of dealing with illness and many people possibly avoiding serious illness because they are more aware of how our mind, body and spirit work in unison.

I also carried out some research for this article and was fascinated when I discovered the study that Dr. James W. Pennebaker carried out, who is a professor at the Department of Psychology at the University of Texas. For over twenty years, he has been giving people that he comes across an assignment, which is, to write down their deepest feelings about an emotional upheaval in their life for 15 to 20 minutes a day, over four consecutive days. His findings showed that most of those who followed his simple instructions discovered that their immune systems strengthened, others saw their grades improve and sometimes entire lives changed. This to me totally affirms my thoughts about the power of writing.

Mental Health

Personally, I know firsthand that writing can help you heal your mind. A few years before I began writing I suffered from post-traumatic stress. This is quite an internal thing that cannot be visually seen on the outside, other than a possible change in social attitude, as it can often make people withdraw themselves from society. I know that this was the situation in my case. I felt that I had to get away from my current situation and I even went so far as to move to the other side of the world. Fortunately, for me this extremity has had a very positive outcome as it has allowed me the space I needed to explore and reconnect with life again. When I started writing, it helped bring me back to myself. I could express things in a way that worked for me. I have shared things that I never thought that I would have been able to and probably would not have shared verbally with anyone. My thoughts feel free and I feel cleansed from any undealt with emotions from the past as writing has given me the ability to release through a different voice.

Anyone wishing to explore the prospect of writing to heal should try out the assignment that Dr. James W. Pennebaker gave to his subjects, which was :

"Over the next four days, write about your deepest emotions and thoughts about that emotional upheaval that has been influencing your life the most. In your writing, really let go and explore the event and how it has affected you. You might tie this experience to your

childhood, your relationship with your parents, people you have loved or love now, or even your career. Write continuously for 20 minutes."

Accompanied with the assignment came some writing tips:

- *Find a time and a place where you won't be disturbed.*
- *Write continuously for at least 20 minutes.*
- *Don't worry about spelling or grammar.*
- *Write only for yourself.*
- *Write about something extremely personal and important for you.*
- *Deal only with events or situations you can handle now.*

Writing has changed my life. I embrace it so much because I now have a passion for it and I know that I will always write to help others, help myself and to be creative. Writing from the heart is powerful and we don't need to be academically gifted to do it (I know that I am certainly not an academic) but I am a person who has a passion for writing and who knows firsthand the benefits of this wonderful divine gift.

I believe so much in the power of writing that I now dedicate my life to it. Through Serenity Press, I have created an avenue, which I can make my words and the words of others available to the world. Through my writing, I want to share love and hope. Through my children's books, I want to share magic.

See more of Karen's articles at
www.buildingbeautifulbonds.com

Sharing your story is all part of the healing process

Karen McDermott

This comment shouted at me from a page recently! Such obvious words but they resonated with me so well. I began writing in 2010 and I have not stopped since. It is not a desire to have my ego given a boost; I write because every time I do I heal and release. When I first began to write it was all very deep and intense, this is what I needed to write to share what I was going through at that time. Now, as I grow, I write differently depending on what I am experiencing and am influenced by at that given time. When I feel inspired my first instinct is to write about it.

This morning I was guided to a blog that was shared by a young Irish man who has suffered from a debilitating depression, the name of his blog is 'Depression is my friend' I did not know what to expect when I first began to read his story but it touched me in so many ways that I could never imagine. It shows me that this young man is coming through and healing as he is sharing his story to help others. This story touched me so deeply that I offered him a chance to feature it in a book I am creating. I connected with this young man's story and courage that he has shared it. I encountered a dark period in my life through and as I emerged out the other side of this dark tunnel I too felt compelled to share my story to maybe touch someone who may need help and hope.

So many people are reserved about sharing their low times when, in fact, it should be encouraged. If more people were brave like Conor I reckon the taboo about mental health would begin to be totally eradicated. It is ok to have a fragile time, it doesn't mean that it is going to be like that forever, people need to know that they will come through and they may even come through a happier, stronger and more empowered version of themselves. People suffering would not feel so alone during what is a life altering time of their lives. It takes strength in abundance to share your story with the world, but is that not what we are supposed to do? Help each other in times of need? So why do so many people feel that they are unable to share, putting these limitations on ourselves is holding back healing, an important part of the process that can free you and guide someone else.

See more of Karen's articles at
www.buildingbeautifulbonds.com

Spiritual Journey

Karen McDermott

If someone had of mentioned to me a Spiritual Journey a few years ago I would have just said "What a load of Mumbo Jumbo". However, after experiencing a life changing transition over the past few years I have never been more at peace with myself. I do not feel that it is necessary to find God or any other godly figure to have a spiritual journey. I feel that it is what happens within one's own soul that changes their outlook on themselves and their place in life itself and all for the better. I have found a peaceful happy place within which I would not swap for all of the money in the world. There can be no price put on it but if its essence could be bottled it would be a heavenly scent. There has been a book written called 'Eat, Pray, Love', which describes one woman's own spiritual journey to happiness within, and it has been a best seller and made into a movie starring Julia Roberts.

Therefore, this goes to show that we can all feel inspired by other people's journeys of self- discovery. Nevertheless, what we need to remember is that it doesn't have to be a dramatic life altering and big family upheaval type of self-journey. We don't all need to dump our hubbies and go travelling we may just need to take time out for ourselves without feeling guilty. Find a balance that works for us, enjoy it, and embrace the changes in your perceptions of the things around you and yourself. Allow your values to alter and your dreams to change. Do not be afraid of the natural process that this journey brings; you will be a more balanced individual because of it, never failing to learn more things and loving each new day that will bring new things your way. If you are aware, you will learn something new every day.

I am lucky that I can say that I truly have found ME. I can now sincerely say that I am deeply happy and fulfilled as a person. Don't get me wrong; I am no saint and I still make mistakes and I learn every day from them but I now have a more positive outlook and I am more aware of others. I feel so privileged to have been given this opportunity to get to where I am now even though OH BOY it has been a rough journey.

Who would have known that the one person who was the cause of such upheaval in my life would actually end up being my saviour? I listened to my intuition, which was shouting loud within 'Through conflict comes change'. I knew things couldn't go on the way they were my life was not my own I lived as a puppet for others. I went with what my heart was telling me and it has worked out for me, it was a gamble but it has paid off. I had to learn something very hard for me as a pleasing Piscean to do which was to say 'Sorry, but NO' without the guilt of feeling that I have let others down. I learned a lot by this alone and I have never looked back. I am now an at home mum and I could not be happier. I have come from being a working hard go-getter trying to make something of myself so that my family would be proud of me whilst also trying to please others constantly. The transition to being proud of me was a challenging one and many instilled values that I was taught throughout my childhood have been changed; they were not all bad but they didn't fit me so I traded them in for some snug fitting values.

We will all eventually get to a crossroads at some point in our lives where we can make the choice to change if we are not happy with how things are going on our life journey or we can choose to stay on the same road. No matter which road we choose there will ultimately be challenges, which we will face, but if we are in touch with ourselves and in a more positive place this will ultimately assist us in dealing with those challenges. It can also mean that we will be happier with less and embrace the things in life, which mean the most to us. I hope everyone gets the opportunity to experience a spiritual journey all of their own because life can mean so much more when we are comfortable in our own skin.

(This was one of the very first articles I wrote)

See more of Karen's articles at
www.buildingbeautifulbonds.com

Beginning to Heal

Christie Lyons

Just a few weeks before Christmas, I lost my baby. The most common term used is miscarriage, or as the hospital called it when they released me from the emergency department, 'spontaneous abortion'. I prefer to refer to it as a baby, because it gives much more meaning to the fact that I lost a living being that was beginning to grow inside of me. It just seems too cold and clinical to call it any of those other medical terms, and considering that carrying a child is such a beautiful and miraculous event, I think it at least deserves the acknowledgement of a more significant term.

After two agonising weeks of constant tests and hospital visits, my husband and I were finally told the news that we were dreading to hear, and I felt like my heart was being ripped out of my chest as the doctor uttered the words. I felt physical pain from the heartbreak I was experiencing and although it was only early on in the pregnancy, it hurt all the same. Our baby was already gone.

Being just eight weeks pregnant when I lost my baby, I honestly struggled at first to allow myself to grieve. I had this inane belief that I wasn't allowed to be so upset because it was so early on in my pregnancy, and being such a common occurrence, I should somehow 'suck it up' and move on because it happened so often. Although I had such a strong support network of friends and family around me, it wasn't until my they were adamant that I stay at home and grieve that I began to allow myself to rightfully be upset about my loss.

During this time at home, I started to research. I needed to know more about why this had happened and looked everywhere I could for answers. I came across several different theories about miscarriage and the reasoning behind it, but the medical answers weren't enough for me. I needed a deeper meaning for my loss. It was during this search for meaning that I came across Karen McDermott's book 'The Visitor'. Her story helped me to grieve, and it allowed me to give the loss of my baby more significance.

As I read Karen's words, I began to feel a connection with her and so I joined the Adopt a Mum network, where I was able to find support from not only Karen, but also a wonderful group of like-minded souls. Although these were people that I had never met, I felt such a sense of comfort among this group and it was thanks to them that my passion for writing was reignited. Karen invited me to contribute my story to her new book that was being published and I felt so honoured that I started working on it straight away.

Through writing, I was able to record all the emotions I had felt throughout the events of my life, and by the time I had reached the loss of my baby, I realised that I was beginning to heal. Writing about my journey was a wonderfully therapeutic process and I was finally able to truly let go of some of my past hurts and negative emotions. I genuinely felt like a brand new person after completing my story. I felt rejuvenated, my hope was renewed, and I was excited about my future. My desire to write had been restored and I began to explore another passion of mine that had gone awry, my spirituality.

The months that have passed since losing this beautiful soul have been nothing short of extraordinary. For the first time in a long time, I feel a newfound confidence and I am genuinely happy. I have been able to focus on my creative interests and have made sure I take time out to do so. My relationships with my husband and family have improved immensely, and every aspect of my life seems to be falling into perfect synchronicity. I have been writing to my heart's content, reading and researching all the many wondrous aspects of the spiritual world, and all the while, everything around me seems to be harmonious.

Although losing my baby was one of the saddest times of my life, I also believe that it happened for a reason. If I hadn't experienced it, I don't believe that I would have explored my past wounds in so much depth, which means that I might not have truly been given the opportunity to heal. I will be forever grateful to my little angel for giving me the chance to start again.

See more of Christie's articles at
www.buildingbeautifulbonds.com

Taking a Risk –
Where I am supposed to be

Christie Lyons

I would like to start by sharing a promise that I made to my late grandfather when he passed in August 2011. As I stood on the pier in St Leonards with my family around me, I read this aloud in honour of him before his ashes were spread into the ocean.

My Promise to You

My Beautiful Pa,

I will always remember the special moments we shared together, the things you've taught me, and the morals and life lessons you have given me.

I will continue to share stories about you, and talk about you, so your memory lives on.

I will always put my family first.

I will remember that even though you're gone, you are still with me, guiding me through my life, and although you can't answer me back when I need you, I know you can hear me and you're there.

I promise to try to live my life to the fullest and appreciate the simple things in life. I will try new things, take risks, and make the most of each day.

I miss you more and more each day, but I know I will see you again someday.

I love you.

Since my youngest son was born in October last year, my whole world has changed, and not just because I had become a Mum again. I'd lived my life for several years, devoting the majority of my time and energy to my career in early childhood and I did so because I was genuinely passionate about my work, and I loved going to work every day. It wasn't until my son Nate was born that my eyes were opened for the first time in a very long time. Up until his birth, I had every intention of taking just four months off for maternity leave, and I was going to head back to work full time and get straight back into the work that I loved.

Nate decided to arrive five weeks early, and although I was prepared to deal with not being able to bring him home right away, as my eldest son Brendon was also premature, I was not prepared for Nate being rushed to the children's hospital to have open-heart surgery at just ten days old. This experience, without a doubt, was the hardest time of my life, and we eventually brought Nate home safe and healthy when he was almost three weeks old. It was while I was carrying him out of the hospital to take him home for the very first time, that I finally realised that I was going to do everything in my power to spend as much time at home as possible, and suddenly my career meant nothing to me.

I spent the next few months absolutely loving every moment of just being 'Mum' and because my eldest son was now ten years old, I had forgotten just how much I appreciated every tiny moment of having a newborn; the way he looks at me when I'm feeding him, his first smile, his smell. I was cherishing every single minute and I didn't want to miss a single thing. I was also beginning to see the positive effects my being at home was having on my eldest son Brendon, and it made me so happy to see how pleased he was to come home from school each day, knowing I was there to greet him. I knew that if I was to return to work when I supposed to, that there would be too many special moments I would miss out on in both my sons' lives, and I was determined to find a way to allow me to stay at home.

In the meantime, being at home meant that I was able to dedicate my time to my other passions; my writing and the Facebook page that my sister in law Jess and I created. With all that I had experienced recently, it fuelled me to focus more on my spiritual journey, and so I began spending more and more time placing my energies into the page, and the beautiful community we had created some several months ago. Living so close by to Jess meant that I was able to visit regularly with Nate during the day, and we would spend hours upon hours working on the page, trying new ideas, and developing our skills. This page that had been created by us to simply allow us to share our spiritual journey with other like-minded people, very quickly started growing and as we spent more time opening up and tapping into our intuition and gifts, we were amazed to realise that we in fact both had much more ability than we first realised.

It didn't take very long at all before we found that we had a waiting list of clients to read for and that our page was so popular among the Facebook community, that it was starting to become a full time job for us both. Every time I would log in to read a message of gratitude or feedback about how accurate we had been, it gave me a warm, fuzzy feeling inside and it began to sink in that this was what I was meant to be doing. Everywhere I looked there was a sign or message pointing me in that direction, and knowing that we were making such a big difference in people's lives, simply by practicing something we were passionate about and loved, was amazing to me. Not only was our page growing, and so were our abilities, but the time spent working on our page has truly brought us together, and I not only view Jess as my sister, but as my most genuine, closest friend.

Another wonderfully inspiring moment occurred for me that kept me engaged in my passion for writing. I had decided to create a photo book of Nate's journey in life so far, as a keepsake to remind not only him, but also our family of his challenging entry into the world. When it arrived, my son Brendon said to me "You should make an actual book out of this". When I questioned him on what he meant by that, he explained, "Well, if you wrote a book about Nate and his heart, it would help other families going through the same thing". Needless to say, I was swelling with pride for my young man for coming up with such a beautiful idea, and so, very shortly afterward, 'Nate's Special Healing Heart' was published, and we now donate all proceeds of the sale of the book to HeartKids.

I began to question whether early childhood was for me anymore, and I spent many hours in a confused state trying to decide which path to take. As my return to work date drew nearer, I started to panic a little bit, knowing that I would be giving up a full time career that paid reasonably well, in order to follow my dreams. It was a very big risk, and something I fought back and forth with in my mind on several occasions. What would we do financially? Why would I give up a wonderful, secure job? I had so many questions, but only I could answer them.

It was one night when I read an email from one of our clients that quite simply said, "Please don't go back to your other job" after having received guidance from me several days prior, that it hit me. This work makes me feel complete and gives me a sense of purpose. I also remembered the promise I had made to my grandfather:

I promise to try to live my life to the fullest and appreciate the simple things in life. I will try new things, take risks, and make the most of each day.

That was it. I had made my decision, and I was going to make it happen. It was as simple as that. It has been one of the best decisions I have ever made and not only am I now able to spend my time and energy on nurturing my children, but I am also in a much happier place, having not even realised until now just how much blissfulness was there waiting for me. I am now able to fully appreciate the saying "You need to close one door before another one opens", as I experience so many more doors opening up for me that I didn't even know existed. I am, without a doubt, where I am meant to be.

See more of Christie's articles at
www.buildingbeautifulbonds.com

Finding Light in a Dark Place

Ella Kate Reeves

Life After Diagnosis

There is no real light without darkness so why negate either when disease has shredded your reality or you are transitioning into a new you?

"People are like stained – glass windows. They sparkle and shine when the sun is out, but when the darkness sets in, their true beauty is revealed only if there is a light from within."

Elisabeth Kubler-Ross

'Beating cancer' (not a phrase I am personally fond of) or any life threatening illness can be physically and emotionally tough, and sometimes the journey doesn't end when you get the all clear. For many people, adjusting to life beyond cancer can be difficult, with a new set of challenges to face. I have broken my experiences into areas I think are significant. From the darkness, you will soon see glimmering stars of enlightenment.

Physical changes

You may also be dealing with some physical changes that have resulted from cancer or cancer treatment. Changes to your body might include hair loss, weight loss or gain, scarring, loss of a limb or loss of a breast (mastectomy), loss of sexual function, or having a colostomy bag.

Whether your body has changed in a way that is visible to others or not, it can be a lot to come to terms with and adapt to. Your body and your appearance can have a big impact on how you feel about yourself and how you think others perceive you. Your self-esteem may have taken quite a knock and this can affect your confidence in a number of ways –for example, at work, in social situations and in your relationships. However, it is possible to come to terms with your body changes.

There is no right or wrong way to feel

Everyone's experience of surviving cancer will feel slightly different; it depends on your personality, personal circumstances and what type of cancer and treatment you have had. For most people, however, it's an emotional experience. Some people feel able to resume their life easily when their cancer treatment finishes and can put the experience behind them. Some are so pleased to have survived cancer that they relish their cancer-free life with renewed vigour. But for many others, the physical and emotional impact of their cancer experience hits home when it's all over. Some people who've experienced cancer report a significant level of anxiety or depression when their treatment is complete. According to Dr. Frances Goodhart, consultant clinical psychologist and author of "The Cancer Survivor's Companion", this is a very natural response. ..."When you find out you have cancer, it can all happen very quickly, the diagnosis followed by treatment decisions is within days ... then you often go through a grueling time getting through the treatments with loved ones and healthcare professionals all around you, helping you through it. It's only afterwards, when your support team has gone and you have the time to think about what you've been through, that you feel the effects."

Fatigue

Cancer and cancer treatments can also leave you feeling fatigued (overwhelmingly tired). According to Dr. Goodhart, "At least three-quarters of people going through cancer treatment say they experience it, and the majority of those continue to feel fatigued after treatment ends." Fatigue can be long-lasting and disrupt many areas of your life, so it's important not to ignore it. Instead, listen to your body and give yourself time to adjust. Dr. Goodhart recommends trying the "3 Ps" - prioritise, plan and pace yourself – as a way of coping until the fatigue starts to lift. Try making a plan each day, prioritising the most important things you would like to achieve, and stick to it. If you find that certain tasks make you feel very tired, pace yourself by reducing the amount you do. At the same time, being physically active can help to reduce your fatigue, if you go about it in the right way. Start with a small amount of physical activity and gradually increase it over time. Don't do more than you feel able to. The type of exercise you choose can also be important.

There really is no light without darkness: Your Emotions

Dark feelings, the desire to hide, give up, check out, withdraw, fall apart and many variants. So why deny any of what you feel, why let your head talk you out of the deepest stirring terror that may arise in relation to facing your own death? Why on earth would any emotionally intelligent and aware person deny what's been dragged to their forefront of reality (often suddenly) after diagnosis, or even remission? You still know it can strike again, you still feel really raw, delicate, shaken and vulnerable. You have just had your world turned upside down.

Talking and support

Not everyone likes to talk about their feelings or how difficult they're finding a situation. If this is you, don't feel obliged to open up. You may find that working through the hard times by yourself or expressing yourself more privately through art or music works best for you. But for many of us, talking to someone about a distressing experience allows us to let off steam, let out difficult feelings, receive support and get a different perspective on things. Who you talk to depends on your circumstances and how you're feeling. Some people are most comfortable with their partner or a close family member, while others find it hard to admit their true feelings and worries to their loved ones.

Dr Goodhart explains: "For some people, talking to someone they're not close to allows them to let their guard down and admit just how tricky it [coping after cancer] is sometimes." You might feel that you would like to talk to a healthcare professional or to people who have been through similar experiences, and there are a number of ways you can find them. You can discuss your feelings and get advice and support from:

- Your cancer care team. When you finish your treatment, they can give you advice on where to go for further support. Depending on your area, they may be able to refer you to a psychologist who specialises in cancer care.

- Support groups – post-cancer support groups are increasingly available and can be a very positive experience for people who attend. These support groups tend to be very informal and provide a place for people to chat, swap experiences and offer advice and support to each other, if they feel like it. It is generally acceptable to just sit and listen if you prefer. Find a group near you.

- Cancer support centres provide relaxed and informal environments to meet other people who have or have had cancer.

- You can also blog about your experiences (I would really encourage a creative outlet of any sort that feels good for you).

Transformation

This requires serious courage and the ability to let go of that which is no longer serving you, and the 'skilful ability' to trust in the unknown/new. The rebirth of another you; a different you; a you that may well be far wiser, juicier, deeper, richer and stronger. True inner strength relies on surrender and rebirth. So let the old you DIE. Why not? The true light shines through darkness. It's so easy to shine in the light of the sunshine when you are well and in your flow, feeling things are under control or this or that….but when that control gets zapped you have to go in. And in you will go, deeply…

Now is the time to see what you are made of and what you may have been missing in life prior to diagnosis. Does that sound odd? 'Why would I have been missing something prior to this grim diagnosis?', I hear many many clients and peers ask.

- All I can share is my experience.
- Small things and big things that supported those shifts.
- What's helped me at my breaking points, my total collapses, breakdowns, urges to quit this wordily pantomime, give up completely (as numbness seemed far preferable than the pain of staying alive and present in my emotions).

This is not a bumper sticker sickly sweet blog. I haven not got the answers of any mass generalisations, but I do have a ton of personal experience that I would like to pass on. You may find that you are trying to cope with anxiety, low mood, depression, anger or a mixture of negative emotions at various times during treatment,surgery and even remission which surprises many. There are many reasons why this might be the case. Dr Goodhart explains: … "It's very common to feel frightened or vulnerable, sad or angry because of what's happened to you. I've known patients to feel lost when their treatment is over and they're no longer getting support from their cancer care team, or lonely because friends and family can be wonderful but they don't always understand the trauma you've been through. And they don't,which is a huge shock in itself….Others are scared to be happy in case the cancer comes back, and it's also common to feel confused about how to fit back into your life because your role and your relationships have had to change during your treatment…. On top of that, people often feel guilty about those feelings because their family and their doctors have worked so hard to get them to that point, and they feel terrible for not feeling as happy as everyone else that they've gotten through it. It's common to put on a front to protect friends and family, and they [cancer survivors] can end up feeling quite isolated.

...Some of these emotions do resolve over time, but time alone is not always the answer. A lot of the distress does fade into the background over time, but you may need to find ways to manage it in whichever way suits you. Everyone is unique in their journey of re-assimilation"....

Recognise what you've been through and how well you have done

- Don't be hard on yourself.

- Give yourself permission to grieve for what you've lost and, if it feels right for you, find someone you feel you can talk to about it.

- Don't avoid the issue – we all avoid doing things we find hard, but by doing so difficult feelings can build up.

- Try to give yourself a goal – something you know you need to do, such as accepting a part of your body that has changed – and gradually build up to it. For example, if you don't want to go out because you're worried about being stared at, start by making a list of things you could say to any comments people might make, and go out with a friend or partner to a local café for 10 minutes. Then increase the length and frequency of your outings.I once nearly had a guy stab me on a bus because I had a swollen upper lip and he presumed it was some kind of filler/botox etc and had judgements and assumptions....I chose to look him straight in the eye and told him about the surgery I'd just undergone (not suggesting that this is necessarily the best way to address difficult and hairy situations like that , however it is the decision I made, at that time.

- Re-build your self-esteem – focus on your achievements and take time to assess all the good things that you have done and still have to offer.

- Learn to trust your body again – Dr Goodhart explains: "Confidence in your own body can be very damaged by cancer. Your body can feel as though it's failed you and can't be trusted. Every twinge may feel like a sign that the cancer has returned. But you can re-learn your body's signals and, in time, start to have confidence in yourself as a 'healthy person' like you did before the cancer."

- Try some exercise – when you feel up to it, regular exercise can help you to combat low mood and help you feel physically stronger. Read more about exercise during and after cancer on the Macmillan website.

- Get further advice on tackling depression, anxiety or anger – if you're struggling or worried, talk to your GP or cancer care team. They can discuss diagnosis and treatment options with you, such as talking therapies and medication.

There are all sorts of support out there but it's not likely to bring light into your dark zones unless you reach out, educate yourself, meet people who have shared experiences and inspire you….allow your tears and vulnerability to flow whenever they come; no judgment, unconditional compassion for what you are grieving, scared of and transforming into.

See more of Ella's work at

www.wateringmysoul.wix.com/ellakatereeves

USEFUL RESOURCES AND LINKS

Beyond Blue

beyondblue is working to reduce the impact of anxiety, depression and suicide in the community by raising awareness and understanding, empowering people to seek help, and supporting recovery, management and resilience.

www.beyondblue.org.au

Headspace – National Youth Mental Health Foundation

Headspace is helping thousands of young people get their lives back on track.

www.headspace.org.au

Black Dog Institute

The Black Dog Institute is a not for profit organisation and world leader in the diagnosis, treatment and prevention of mood disorders such as depression and bipolar disorder.

www.blackdoginstitute.org.au

Building Beautiful Bonds

buildingbeautifulbonds.com has been created as a positive communication tool for connecting women of all ages.

www.buildingbeautifulbonds.com

Soul Sistas Healing & Guidance

Jess and Christie are on a journey of spiritual discovery and are eager to share their knowledge and experiences with you. Their mission is to promote and encourage healing and guidance for others on the journey of their soul.

www.soulsistashealing.com

White Light Publishing House

White Light Publishing House aspires to share inspiration, guidance and love with the world, and to heal the mind, body and soul with words.

www.whitelightpublishingau.com

Official Author Website – Ella Kate Reeves

Ella Kate Reeves is a movement and dance therapist and an accredited psychotherapist. When illness struck, leaving her unable to dance, she wrote. Life has seen many challenges come her way. She shares these challenges through her unique poetry collection.

www.wateringmysoul.wix.com/ellakatereeves

White Light Publishing House

www.whitelightpublishingau.com

www.facebook.com/whitelightpublishinghouse

www.ingramcontent.com/pod-product-compliance
Lightning Source LLC
Chambersburg PA
CBHW071907290426
44110CB00013B/1313